12 Steps: The Sequel

By:

Wendy Ellen Coughlin, PhD

BALBOA.
PRESS

A DIVISION OF HAY HOUSE

ISBN: 978-1-4525-5075-6 (sc)
ISBN: 978-1-4525-5074-9 (e)
ISBN: 978-1-4525-5073-2 (hc)

Library of Congress Control Number: 2012907797

Balboa Press books may be ordered through booksellers or by contacting:

Balboa Press
A Division of Hay House
1663 Liberty Drive
Bloomington, IN 47403
www.balboapress.com
1-(877) 407-4847

Printed in the United States of America

Balboa Press rev. date: 7/16/2012

For my children

Our deepest fear is not that we are inadequate.

Our deepest fear is that we are
powerful beyond measure.

It is our light, not our darkness
that most frightens us.

We ask ourselves, Who am I to be brilliant, gorgeous,
talented, fabulous? Actually, who are you not to be?

(Williamson, 1992)

Contents

Took a searching inventory of our assets, talents and capabilities.

You've seen the bad and the ugly, now evaluate the good. What talents lay dormant during your addiction that can now be developed?

Admitted to God, to ourselves and another human being the exact nature of our potential as sober individuals.

Our secrets can limit us; if no one knows we have talents and abilities, the expectations remain low. Share your dreams and they may become manifest.

Identified our characteristics, skills and talents that can now be put to good use.

List your assets and prioritize those that will give you the most joy and fulfillment.

Humbly asked God to guide and support our future development.

Be prepared to receive support and guidance; be open to possibilities.

Made a list of goals and plans we envision for our future.

Develop a road map. Without a destination, you won't arrive.

PREFACE

This book is targeted to people who have worked the original 12 steps, as outlined in the book, *Alcoholics Anonymous* (Alcoholics Anonymous World Services, Inc., 2001), for two or more years.

For Newcomers: You may wish to put this book down and pick up the basic text for the 12 step program you belong to before continuing here.[1] Like most sequels, the writings here will have more meaning if you have completed the original.

For Professionals: This can be an extremely valuable tool for your clients who have multiple years of recovery but feel the original 12 steps and "those meetings" just do not help anymore. That is, of course, malarkey, but that is the reason for this book. What follows represents the other side of the coin, a positive spin on the original 12 steps. The original 12 steps focus on recovering from the wreckage of addiction. Eventually, if someone is thorough, those negative elements either disappear or are so minimal they hardly warrant attention. There is a spiritual awakening, a rebirth. Recovery continues beyond abstinence toward maximum wellness. That is the time to apply the concepts of *The Sequel*.

For all others: Enjoy! Be challenged. Consider your potential. Recovery allows you to discover untapped abilities as well as resurrect old skills and talents. It is an opportunity to strengthen skills, develop new goals, and take risks. If you have already beaten the odds and established multiple years of abstinence, you have already proven you have the discipline, faith and perseverance to achieve any goal you set. As Dr. Seuss said:

You have brains in your head,

You have feet in your shoes,

You can steer yourself

any direction you choose. (Seuss, 1990)

How to start? Read on! And, by all means, KISMIF! (Keep It Simple, Make It Fun)

INTRODUCTION

12 Steps: The Sequel provides guidelines to continue recovery past abstinence into maximal living. Using the principles of the original steps, *The Sequel* promotes continual growth and personal development. As you work the Sequel steps², you can admit you have the power to manage your life and have been restored to sanity. Once you identify your assets, talents and capabilities, you can develop a plan to fulfill your potential. You will develop new goals, goals that provide maximum benefit for yourself and others. Ultimately, you will enjoy another level of spiritual experience – one emanating from the awakened spirit that is within you.

In 1980 I felt hopeless. I was about to be evicted and my car was being repossessed. I had already lost my job, destroyed my credit and alienated my friends. I had been in a self-destructive pattern of addictive behavior since adolescence. I was a shell of a person. I made plans for my suicide but then had another thought – what if the problem was drinking and drugging? *Perhaps I should try recovery before death.* I called a 12 Step hotline and the journey began. Sobriety felt as if I was living on a parallel planet, everything was the same yet somehow totally different. The first few years I relied on others to guide my recovery. The journey was not an easy one, but there was steady progress. I knew I could not turn back. I did not know how to live but I knew I did not want to die. I am immensely grateful to the 12-step fellowships for giving me the support and direction I needed to stay clean and sober. Many years later, I have more blessings than I can count. Reflecting back, it is clear that my success was the result of working the original 12 steps. First I worked the original 12 steps to recover from addiction, then the Sequel steps to reach my fullest potential. This book describes the path from hopeless despair in addiction to flourishing in recovery.

Getting sober[3], becoming free of addictive behavior, can be a scary thing. Every moment of every day holds new challenges as you learn to live life on life's terms. To stay present, and not escape into addictive behaviors, takes an immense amount of effort. Just about everything in life changes. Some changes may be relatively minor, for example, changes in physical appearance. A former compulsive over-eater will certainly be changing clothing sizes and styles. A recovering alcoholic's hygiene and grooming will improve. An addict in recovery will maintain eye contact. On a larger scale, jobs, living situations and social networks change as addicts emerge from the drug culture, the bar, the kitchen or the racetrack. Some changes will be all-encompassing, impacting virtually every area of one's life. Every change reflects the transformation that accompanies recovery from addiction.

Addiction is a biopsychosocial disease process. On a biological level, food and drugs (including the drug, alcohol) change the way we feel frequently interfering with our cognitive process. Mood-altering substances prevent us from truly experiencing the world. Behavioral addictions like gambling and sex disrupt our ability to think; the compulsive quest for arousal distracts attention from all other aspects of our lives. The impact of using substances or compulsively engaging in certain behaviors often obliterates our ability to manage day-to-day events. We learn to disregard ourselves as well as others.

We escape reality. Why else would anyone engage in illegal, physically damaging, compulsive behaviors? To change how we feel - is that not escaping reality? For conviviality? Man is a social animal, we do not need substances to engage with others.

As a result of our history of escaping reality, we seldom know how to deal with reality! No matter our age, education or experience, those of us who have suffered addictive illness come into recovery with very few tools for sober living. Take, for example, the chronic opiate addict, an individual who has been able to put aside virtually every aspect of responsibility to self and others during his/her addiction. If the addiction has been of any duration, getting clean often entails a disaster-recovery plan. Typically, family, finances, career, and health have been abandoned. The very process of moving out of addictive behavior seems overwhelming and nearly impossible. For those that are successful in maintaining abstinence, it may seem enough to accomplish that one feat alone in a lifetime. Shouldn't we relax and simply enjoy our recovery? For some, getting clean and staying clean is a full time job; it is such a relief that it is reward enough. If this is you, enjoy your recovery. If, on the other hand, you feel incomplete, as if being clean and sober alone is not enough – read on! Your newfound freedom and happiness may provide the energy and opportunity to continue growing and changing your life.

The next 12 chapters take you through the 12 steps re-interpreted for growth in recovery. When working the original 12 steps, we painstakingly address many faults and weaknesses by looking at our defects of character and making amends. The 10th step states that it is a "spiritual axiom that every time we are disturbed…there is something wrong *with us."* (Alcoholics Anonymous World Services, Inc., 2001, p. 90). The steps help us to recover from our addictive history and all the associated misdeeds. Recovery focuses, of necessity, on the negative aspects of our past. This book uses the same basic steps to focus on our strengths in order to enhance our future.

In 1958 Bill Wilson, a co-founder of the Alcoholics Anonymous program, wrote a letter to the AA community that was published in the *Grapevine* magazine (Wilson, 1958). The letter refers to "emotional sobriety" as "the development of much more real maturity and balance." He infers that the quest for emotional sobriety may be the next major spearhead for AA and questions, "How to translate a right mental conviction into a right emotional result, and so into easy, happy and good living." The way to do that is to commit to a life that maximally fulfills our capabilities. Abraham Maslow, founder of the humanistic psychology movement, identified the drive to fulfill one's potential as a motivating factor impelling individuals to move forward. In his 1954 book, *Motivation and Personality* (Maslow, 1954), he explains that after people fulfill their "deficiency needs" they move beyond them toward self-actualization. People in recovery are no different than anyone else. When we work the 12 steps, we resolve our deficiencies and establish a strong foundation for continued recovery. After a few years abstinence alone may not be enough. Often, there is an urge to do more and be more. We need to continue growing, changing, and improving our lives so we can enjoy happy and good living. Many books have been written on happiness and optimal experience. The need to find meaning and purpose in life is a prerequisite for optimal living.

The *12 Step Sequel* re-applies the original[4] 12-step principles to guide this process. With the exception of the 3rd and 11th steps, which are the spiritual foundation of any 12 step program, the steps are re-worded to reflect the potential for growth in recovery. *We admitted we were powerless - that our lives have become unmanageable* is transformed into **We admitted we now have the power to manage our lives.** *Came to believe that a power greater than ourselves could restore us to sanity* becomes **Having been restored to sanity we continued to improve our lives.**

No need to learn something new, go to therapy (although that might help speed the process), find a new group, join a new religion (also something that might help); simply use the 12 Steps that have already been working in your life. Take each step and reframe it in a positive direction. I offer some options here but the exact wording is not important. The concept is critical. By using the Sequel Steps to develop your skills and talents, you will find meaning and purpose in life. With continued growth you will enjoy an even greater freedom and happiness than you have experienced thus far.

And will you succeed?

Yes! You will, indeed!

(98 and ¾ percent guaranteed.)

(Seuss, 1990)

And do not forget along the way, KISMIF! (Keep It Simple, Make It Fun)

Step 1$_S$

Admitted we now have power to manage our lives.

Having had a spiritual awakening as the result of the 12 steps, we establish our recovery and gain strength. We have the power to manage our own lives.

To arrive at this point, we first have to remove the barricades which block our journey. We do that through taking the steps. First, we admit our powerlessness so we can stop the self-defeating cycle of trying to control something over which we have long since lost control. We recognize the unmanageability in our lives and begin to restore organization and order. Looking back on experiences during active addiction, most recovering people discover many examples of insane thinking and behavior. Compulsivity typically has overridden reason and logic. Our minds become clear as we become less driven by obsession and better able to see alternatives. Reviewing the past, we may be overwhelmed with grief and regret that our lives contained so many mistakes. So we take an inventory and share it with another human being. By doing the 5th step most of us learned we were not unique. What we had done was not so bad that we cannot heal and move forward. Being so encouraged, we identify our shortcomings and become committed to changing them. We may feel guilt over things we have said or done in the past. Guilt is appropriate if you have done something wrong, but it is not necessary to languish in guilt. The 8th and 9th steps provide guidance on how to make amends to those we had harmed. Once the first 9 steps are completed to the best of our ability, we can move forward with a clear, if not clean, slate. To safeguard against repeating past inappropriate behavior, we use the 10th step to stay vigilant and correct mistakes as we make them. To assure that our self-will does not run riot again, we continue to seek guidance through prayer and meditation. Feeling blessed to have found a new way of living, we share the gifts of the 12 step program with others. Practicing the principles of the steps bolsters and solidifies sober living.

But how do we translate right mental conviction into right mental result and get off the merry-go-round? We know what not to do. We cannot drink, use drugs, abuse our bodies with food or exercise, gamble, shop, hoard, work, or do anything so compulsively and addictively that it interferes with our day-to-day life. By completing the 12 steps many of us experience "the final agony of seeing how absolutely wrong we have been." (Wilson, 1958)

The first step is to admit we now have power to manage our lives. This might seem risky business for those whose megalomania had previously deluded them into thinking they were doing well, when in reality their addictive illness was bringing them closer to the precipice which ultimately led to their complete defeat. It is a risky endeavor; therefore, I recommend you only attempt this next phase of recovery after you have completed the original 12 steps with a sponsor. A sponsor provides support and objectivity. When dealing with our own issues (past, present, or future), it is best to seek an external perspective, an opinion from an outsider. A sponsor can help assure you have taken a searching inventory, identified the exact nature of your wrongs, and made the necessary amends. Completing the 12 steps of recovery allows you to let go of the past. The steps provide the basic foundation to live life on life's terms. You may wish to wait two or more years to ensure you are comfortable with the many changes that accompany abstinence before adding complexity to your recovery.

Foundations are critical. Without a firm foundation future recovery may teeter, develop a sinkhole or collapse. A building foundation supports the structure of the building. It supports the addition of floors, walls, pipes, electricity, furnishings etc. enabling the building to be fully functional. Recovery requires similar foundations to assure success. Sobriety is supported by a stable living situation, a regimen of self care that includes good nutrition and exercise, and daily social activities. It is also necessary to ensure a flow of sufficient financial resources to meet basic needs. In the world of finance, foundation refers to a funding source providing resources to support the operation of an institution. In recovery a financial foundation can be employment, social services, or loans to re-establish stability. The term, foundation, also refers to the basis on which something is founded. For example, our educational foundation is the basic skill set of reading, writing, and arithmetic. In recovery the 10th, 11th, and 12th steps provide the basic tools for moving forward. You need to have a foundation, in every sense of the word, in order to build sober relationships, families, and careers.

Admitting we have power and can manage our lives is the most important step to future growth and development. If we do not believe we have the power to change our lives, we cannot envision new possibilities. We remain dependent on others, subject to external influences. There is a tendency to overlook personal needs and goals. Self-seeking is suspect. Selfish self-seeking indeed is dangerous; the addict seeking only to promote his or her own agenda is at risk of relapse. Self-centered seeking is, however, a necessity for a fulfilling life. To be self-centered means to have an understanding of who you are, what you can do, and what is important to you. Only through self-discovery can you begin to build on the foundation of sobriety. In recovery we can listen to our inner voices. Having been restored to sanity, it is ok to trust ourselves.

But how do we know if our perceptions are accurate? We need discernment: the ability to see and understand people, places, and things clearly. We must develop insight and the ability to make good judgments. This may take some practice. It is important to honor our individual perspectives; however, we must remain cognizant that our perceptions may be distorted. This is why sponsorship is equally important in working the Sequel as it is in early recovery. Sequel sponsors help guide you through the steps offering experience, strength and hope. They provide feedback, validating and/or challenging your perceptions. Sequel sponsors are life coaches who affirm our growth while helping us stay focused. As you work Step 1_S and begin to manage your life, you are likely to see many new possibilities.

Step 1_S asks you to admit you have the power. Survey your resources now that you are in recovery. At whatever level we enter this next stage in our recovery, we will have the tools to move forward if we have been searching and fearless in working the original 12 steps. But first things first! Do you have the means, the finances (literal and figurative), to support a new self? If you do not, give the miracle a chance to happen and it will. The person who comes into the rooms, homeless, ill and estranged from family can fund his or her new life with a fellowship to provide familial support. Once clean and sober, most find shelter and can maintain a home. Shelter and safety must be established before anyone can tend to personal growth. Sobriety provides an opportunity to manage your life and improve your resources.

As indicated above, you must have a firm foundation for your recovery in order to successfully move forward. Although 12 step groups are not designed to address any of these peripheral issues, the meetings are usually full of people who have had similar struggles. Draw from the experience, strength and hope of others in recovery. The 9th step promises in the Big Book of Alcoholics Anonymous make it clear that working the steps brings many new perspectives and opportunities (Alcoholics Anonymous World Services, Inc., 2001, pp. 83-84). Working the steps, talking with others, and establishing oneself in a recovering community provide options and alternatives. Few, if any, sincerely working a recovery program fail to find adequate shelter within the first year of sobriety.

If your family of origin is not available to provide support, your "family of choice" will be. Family of choice is a term that defines individuals you choose to bring into your intimate circle, people that function in familial roles. Sponsors, grand-sponsors, sobriety sisters and brothers frequently fill in the gaps left when members from your family of origin are not available. Families estranged due to addiction are often re-united in recovery. Having seen the progress inherent in working the 12 steps, family members may again be available to provide encouragement and guidance. You may find you have incredible power to manage your life when surrounded by both family-of-origin and family-of-choice members.

Once a physical and social foundation is established, the financial foundation must be stabilized. Typically this includes finding or maintaining employment. If you are one of the fortunate few for whom financial support is not an issue that is wonderful. If, however, you need to strengthen your financial reserves, now is the time to do so. Once basic sobriety is established, you may be ready for new training, a new position, or simply to ask for a raise. For some, addiction has destroyed their professional standing, perhaps stripped them of credentials and the ability to continue their careers. Recovery offers the opportunity to re-establish your credibility in all areas, including work. Having the power to manage your life includes the power to restore your professional integrity.

In 12-step groups you will find others who have gone before you and can guide and assist in the tasks at hand. You are no longer alone, isolated in a progressively debilitating disease process. You are surrounded by others who are establishing themselves in recovery and the world. All you have to do is surrender, then you can go on to win. By admitting powerlessness over addictive disease recovery can begin. Once recovery is established, you regain power. The insanity of addiction is in the past and sanity is now restored.

Step 1$_s$ Considerations

1. Have you finished the original 12 steps?

2. Are you ready to begin working the Sequel steps? Have you admitted you have the power to manage your own life?

3. What foundation has been set? What tools are at your disposal to expand your recovery?

4. Do you have a sponsor, life coach, or therapist who supports the concepts of the Sequel?

5. Is there any area of your life that remains unmanageable to the degree that it might interfere with your success in completing the Sequel?

Step 2ₛ

Having been restored to sanity we continued to improve our lives

Coming out of the fog of addictive behavior, we look back and see the insanity of our lives. Fortunately, the 12 steps help us deal with our past. We admit we are powerless, develop a faith that things can change, confess our sins, make amends and move forward. For those whose violations were in absolute contradiction to their values, the journey can be a bit more challenging. Many struggle to overcome the image they see of their addict selves. We know the stigmas that are attached to sexual addiction, drug abuse, hoarding and alcoholism, in 12-step fellowship we usually let go of those social concerns. Our inter-personal (interactions between self and others) discomforts are healed through our connection with other addicts. We learn that we all suffered a touch of insanity at one time or another. But there may also be an intra-personal (within the self) conflict. The contradictions between our personal values and past behavior may trigger emotions ranging from mild upset to disgust. It is life changing to rectify the discrepancy between how we see ourselves and what we have done under the influence. Intra-personal conflicts often require more individualized work and may be the domain of psychotherapists skilled in treating addictions[5]. They can help deepen our understanding that addiction leads to insane thinking and, as a result of that insanity, we were not able to control our actions. A skilled therapist will help us update the data banks and look at who we are today. Once abstinent, we can recognize and control our behavior. *We are responsible people.*

Being restored to sanity, the fear of impending doom vanishes. We are cognizant of our behavior in all our affairs. We remember what we have done and what we have said. We are able to follow through on plans. We can begin to dream. We can believe in a future. We have hope. At this point we can venture towards goals; we can trust ourselves in a way we never could while using. Now what?

Depending on how long you were in active addiction and when that addiction took over your life, you may or may not have a career, home and relationships already in place. Since many enter recovery with careers decimated, homes lost and relationships destroyed, it is wise to start with a survey of what is left. Inventory what God gave you, what you have left and what has been taken away.[6] You will find that there are many new opportunities open to you in recovery but first there may be things that you wish to recapture.

Have you lost something or someone that you wish to regain? If so, please work with a sponsor, close friends and family members. It is always helpful to consult others in these matters since friends and family can provide more objective perspectives. There may be benefit to resurrecting previously discarded opportunities. If so, use this step to launch your journey toward restoring those elements damaged by your addiction. If you have lost something integral to your life's satisfaction, pursue it with intention. Do not concede until you have done everything in your power to restore what was lost! This is particularly important with family matters and avocations.

If you have lost professional standing, been humiliated in personal relationships, or ruined your credit, remember: you are a new person and therefore *the past no longer predicts the future*. You are restored to sanity; you are not doing the same thing over and over and expecting different results. You are different today and the impact of what you do will be different. As a recovering person your perspective changes, you have more understanding, patience and tolerance as you approach the future. Most people will see that you are different. Only those most severely damaged by your past behavior will reject a sincere effort to make amends. If that is the case, it is best to move forward recognizing that, as a sane person, you will not repeat that past. Similarly, some violations during our using days prevent a return to certain occupations. This is particularly true when our addictions led to legal difficulties. Some, but not all, licensed professions prohibit a reinstatement of professional credentials to those with felony charges. Before giving up the hope of returning to a career check out the regulations. You will be surprised at how many professional groups have procedures in place to help a previously disabled person restore their credentials.

For those whose addiction may have prevented them from achieving professional or career status, the world is an open field now that you are in recovery. You can do anything you might envision, provided you have the basic inclination or skill for that activity. Sanity means being sensible; a sane person would not choose to go to medical school when he or she struggles with math and science and is over 50 years of age – that would not be a realistic goal. I have met several people, however, who were good in math and science and did complete medical school after age 50. *You will see it when you believe it*. If it is important to you, set your sights on it and move forward.

Occasionally people in recovery are hesitant to take risks. Sometimes this fear emanates from a desire to stay safe. Addiction may have beaten you up and it may seem insane to move into uncharted territory now that you have finally landed in the safe haven of a recovery fellowship. If that is your situation, perhaps you are not ready to move forward. Enjoy the safety of recovery for a while. Take your time; just be careful that you do not "rest" too long. Years ago I had a friend in recovery that was prone to "resting." She knew what she was doing, she was settling for "good enough." She knew she needed to move forward but, for a variety of reasons, she was reluctant to do so. When she became frustrated with her own lack of progress she would share this with her home group. Once she admitted her resistance to claiming the power to manage her life in recovery, it propelled her forward. By acknowledging her lack of growth, she took back her power and recommitted to reaching her goals. More on this in Chapter 5.

When we rest a lot, nothing really changes. At some point, most of us become tired of doing the same thing over and over. Some blame the program, thinking they have outgrown the 12 step fellowships questioning, "Is that all there is?" The answer, of course, is a resounding, "No!" Once we have recovered a reasonable homeostasis (usually after 2 – 3 years of abstinence), we typically experience a consensual reality. Unlike our perception during our using days, we see and experience the world like those around us. We develop routines and are able to follow them, something often impossible during active addiction. Routines allow us to simplify activities of daily living and organize our lives. Our new found efficiency in handling day-to-day matters provides opportunity for new adventures. The purpose of this book is to point out how we can continue to use the 12 steps to move forward in our lives. The fellowship changes its role from houseboat to life raft. We still need to keep it available 24 hours a day, 7 days a week in case we need support, but we no longer need to live in it.

So where do we start? The answer is simple – anywhere. Great, you say, that gives me no clue. Actually, you do not need a clue from outside yourself, this is an inside job. Simply begin. Start with the obvious; what part of your life in recovery is most dissatisfying? If you start with what bothers you the most, you will be highly motivated to make the necessary changes. If your physical condition needs improving, start an exercise program. If your living environment is uncomfortably reminiscent of addiction – clean it up, redecorate, or move. Perhaps it is your job which is unfulfilling; now is the time to pursue more rewarding career opportunities. Most of us have had disruptions in our family and social lives. There is likely much more work needed to have satisfying and fulfilling relationships. If family stress continues to distract you from your individual pursuits, work to heal those relationships before starting a new adventure.

In admitting we have been restored to sanity we let go of the excuses. We admit we have the power to manage our lives. Knowing we have made mistakes or taken detours in the past, we should seek some outside help or guidance. At this juncture, we can once again **make a decision to turn our will and our lives over to the care of God as we understand God.**

Step 2_S Considerations

1. Have you accepted the insanity of your past addictive behavior?

2. Do you believe you have been restored to sanity? What are your expectations of yourself?

3. Have you recovered the important things that were lost? If there are things you cannot recover, have you accepted those losses?

4. What immediate changes do you want to make?

5. What are your dreams for the future?

Step 3$_S$

Made a decision to turn our will and our lives over to the care of God *as we understood God.*[7]

The third step in the Sequel is the same as the original step. Step 3 opens up infinite possibilities if we turn our life over to the care of God. This may seem to contradict step 1$_S$ which says we have power to manage our lives. If we have the power, why turn over our will? Having power does not suggest we should myopically go about directing our life without input from anyone else. Only the most grandiose of narcissists would dare to suggest he or she can do everything alone and do it optimally. By practicing the 3rd Step, we move beyond the limits of self. This step simply suggests we consider alternatives, let go of our egocentric view of the world and explore new directions. We no longer have to be limited by what we see or imagine.

Air travel is an example of practicing the Third Step, letting go and turning our will and our life over to something and/or someone else. People turn their will and their lives over to the care of others every day. Anyone who uses public transportation, drives across bridges or turns on an electric switch is relying on someone or something else to provide support and oversight. Take, for example, air travel. When we travel on a commercial airline, we prepare for the trip with the expectancy that we will reach our destination. Although most travelers have no direct involvement with the design and manufacturing of the aircraft, servicing at the airport or the airline schedule, we comfortably purchase tickets and assume we will arrive at our intended destinations. Few pay attention to the type of aircraft they will be traveling in; even fewer consider the maintenance requirements for the aircraft. We trust the plane is structurally and mechanically sound, we let go and let the FAA[8] handle it. Going to the gate, we generally expect the plane to depart as scheduled. We board with coffee, reading material and neck support, take our seat, and travel across many miles in a short period of time while exerting virtually no personal effort. Every time we board a commercial flight we are, in fact, turning our will and our lives over to powers greater than ourselves. Some will contend that air travel can be understood in concrete, scientific terms while God cannot. To a degree they are correct but, for most of us, the dynamics of flight and the processes required to provide flights are no more understandable than a God concept. Neither can be fully understood except perhaps by the most expert individuals. We may reassure ourselves that the aeronautical engineer understands flight and the mechanisms of an aircraft, but is that really so different from believing that a priest, rabbi or shaman understands God? Clergy attribute the changes in our lives to part of an intricate, divine plan. Is that really so different from the engineer attributing flight to the intricate mechanisms of a plane?

Our attitude towards air travel parallels faith in other ways as well. Most people accept flying as safe and certain. They feel comfortable assuming they will reach their destination and make life plans accordingly. On a day-to-day basis, we simply trust the aircraft will stay in the air bringing us to our destinations without crashing. Our ability to take commercial flights relies on our ability to turn our will and our lives over to a power greater than ourselves and, in doing so, we are often happier and less fearful. When all goes well, we enjoy the benefits of air travel. However, when there is an incident that disrupts plane schedules or threatens lives, everyone begins to re-evaluate their assumptions. News of terrorist activity, severe weather or a plane's mechanical failure creates doubt regarding security and predictability. People question the wisdom of relying on TSA[9] and the FAA, powers greater than themselves. This is not unlike people questioning the existence and power of God when bad things happen.

One thing is certain, if we have faith it is a lot easier to move about in the world. Faith in the vast powers behind air travel allows us to move about the globe. Faith in a God of our understanding allows us to move about our world. In both cases, we make many assumptions and overlook many risks; to do otherwise would paralyze us with fear. By believing in the capability of airlines and pilots, we can fly with assurance. By believing in the capability of a God, we can move forward in our lives without fear. By letting go of fear, we can enjoy new adventures.

The Third Step assures us we do not have to go it alone. It is logical to seek guidance as we move forward. If we approached recovery alone, recognizing the immensity of the task and being aware of the risks and complexities of our lives, it would be immobilizing. The third step suggests we let go of self-will and make a decision to "turn our will and our lives over;" it allows us to admit there is something or someone outside our selves and to access information and support from that source. Step 3 recommends you accept the *care* of God; it does not ask you to relinquish control or power. "Care" implies supervision and assistance, not management. In working the Third Step we choose to allow other information, guidance from a power greater than ourselves, to influence our will and our lives.

There are many definitions of the word "will," most suggest expectancy, intent, or choice. When we say something will happen, there is a sense of inevitability. By this definition turning our will over indicates our lives may not be fated to a certain destiny. Rather than doggedly rushing forward, creating a life of self-fulfilled prophecies, we let go of our individual, sometimes limited, perspectives. We are open to other influences and become teachable. We commit to moving beyond our selves. We accept that someone or something can guide us. By letting go of expectancy, we release our future to many possibilities.

Turning our intent/will over means we stop blindly steering the ship. We become willing to use maps and other tools to guide our navigation. We pay attention to our surroundings and are willing to adjust our course. This is particularly important in early recovery. Our old maps were restricted to places we could go while in our addiction. The destinations we set out towards while "under the influence" are generally quite different from those we might choose in recovery. By letting go of our old intentions, we can write new scripts and plot courses to new destinations!

In recovery we can change course, add new adventures, and often achieve goals we would not dream of in our addiction. Our choices are not limited if we practice the Third Step. By turning our will/choice over to the care of God as we understand God, we open our options to infinite alternatives. We engage in a world beyond ourselves.

Addictive illness isolates its victims from self and others, while recovery reconnects. We connect with others and escape isolation. Early recovery is very much a process of "re-covering" lost elements of day-to-day life. Many of us feel like babies[10], or at least adolescents, learning for seemingly the first time how to manage life on life's terms. The Third Step encourages us to let the God of our understanding guide our lives, just what we need at just the right time. As the fog lifts and sanity returns, life can feel overwhelming. Whether we give in or cave in, it is the **gift of desperation** (God) that typically propels us forward. The Third Step provides a solution to the uncertainties and confusion of early recovery. Having been beaten down by addiction we are desperate for guidance and direction. The **gift of desperation** (God) allows us to reach out for someone or something to care for us and guide us. 12 Step groups provide people to help. AA members have been described as a **group of drunks** (God). Those "**groups of drunks**" become the g-o-d to whom some turn their will and their lives over. Because we have the **gift of desperation**, we can turn our will and our lives over to a **group of drunks**. Simple but not easy!

The proverbial elephant in Step 3 is the word, "god". Yep, it is just a word. Why do we get so disturbed when it is used? Why must we argue so about what it means? In the United States in 1939 (when the steps were first published), it was unlikely that the term God would be used to identify anything other than a Christian concept of a deity. Bill and Bob (the founders of AA) were heavily influenced by the Oxford Group,[11] their use of the term, God, appears to refer to a concept based in Christianity. However, in their infinite wisdom, the founders allowed for multiple definitions of the word," god", by adding the phrase, *"as we understood Him."*

Defining God as a group of drunks: What better "god" to turn our defeated and deflated selves over to than a group of drunks in recovery? This is particularly true for the addicts whose primary addiction was to alcohol. While this may make the most sense to those recovering from alcoholism, others can also benefit from the support found in the rooms of AA. Dr. George Valliant, after years of research and study in the field of alcoholism, recognized the amazing support network and mental health benefits inherent in AA. He noted that those who have recovered from alcoholism were blessed to qualify for membership in AA.[12] Any who have attended a 12 step group are likely to understand the benefits of belonging. A **group of drunks** recovering in AA has survived a potentially fatal illness, worked the 12 steps and found ways of handling life on life's terms. They are likely to have found a new freedom and a new happiness. This is certainly a group of individuals who can help a newcomer learn a better way of living.

*Defining God as **good orderly direction**:* This definition can apply to a deistic god or an atheistic god. Seeing the word as an acronym, g-o-d may be interpreted as "good orderly direction." Who can argue with that? If your god is not a "Him" or a "Her", then maybe it represents ethical and organized guidelines for living. And, if the God of your understanding is a more traditional one, it is likely a God-centered life would also be one of good orderly direction.

*Seeing God as meaning **grow or die**:* Defining g-o-d as "grow or die" is a no-brainer for anyone who has been caught in the web of addiction. If you recognize that the same person will drink, drug, gamble, shop, compulsively work, etc. then you know that to recover you must change. The only logical change that will move you away from addictive behavior is to grow. Grow in social and family relationships. Grow in educational pursuits. Grow in adaptability. Grow older rather than die. For some, early recovery is a very difficult period. If we do not grow personally and spiritually, we may stagnate, wither and die in a symbolic sense of the term. Death may be interpreted as a spiritual or emotional death. Death is the absence of life, life refers to far more than a body breathing and a heart pumping. Life is about growing and changing.

*Seeing God as a **glimpse of destiny**:* Ah, turn your will and your life over as you get a glimpse of destiny – why not? Recovery brings new ideas and perspectives. Participation in 12-step rooms opens new vistas. As members share their experience, strength and hope, they get to eavesdrop on how others live their lives and can discover new options. 12-step rooms around the world allow anyone who wants to attend the opportunity to get a glimpse of what a life in recovery can offer. Getting a glimpse is like seeing the brass ring on the merry-go-round; there is a prize you can catch if you jump on and make a sufficient effort.

Theist, atheist and agnostic

The theist believes in the existence of a deity, a force responsible for the creation and governance of the universe. People have waged wars and fought for different definitions of their deity, but the common thread is a being or beings that are supernatural and super powerful. Often these concepts include omnipresent omnipotence. Many have prescribed definitions and rules that their god(s) follow. Some have names, even if those names cannot be uttered or written, and some are references to natural forces. Whatever one's concept of a deity is, there is definitely a sense of a being that can and will guide and direct your life. Hallelujah! For theists it should be easy to turn one's will and one's life over to the care of God as they understand God. God is defined and perceived to have all power. It should be safe for someone who has been powerless to rely on a power greater than oneself!

The atheist has a rather different challenge with Step 3. If you do not believe in the presence of a deity, denying any form of being that may be the creator or governor of the world, what can you turn your will and your life over to? This is where some of the above definitions come in handy. If g-o-d is a group of drunks, good orderly direction or a glimpse of destiny, there should be no issue with turning one's will and one's life over. Please do not get hung up on the anthropomorphic language, interpret Step 3 in general terms – there is more to life than you!

Agnostics may simply avoid defining this "god" concept when practicing this step. Agnostics are unwilling to state an opinion regarding the existence or non-existence of God. No need to define God if you are not sure he/she/it exists. That still leaves the problem of turning your will and your life over to the care of something that may not be there. Consider the first paragraph of this chapter again – it is more about letting go of your agenda than being cared for. Turning your will and your life over is about getting out of the driver's seat and going along for the ride. If you are not rigidly focused on driving, you can observe the scenery, are likely to see many new things and perhaps explore new roads that pop up along the way. To quote a gruff, old recovering alky from Baltimore City's Chip House, "The only thing you need to know about God is you ain't it!"[13]

Third step debates can go on ad nauseam but to do so only delays progress. As long as you know you are not God and you can turn your will and your life over to something loosely defined as g-o-d, there is a good chance Step 3 can provide solace and relief. For many, working this step leads to changes beyond their wildest dreams. Most people who trust in a power greater than themselves are happier, more successful and less fearful. Why not try it?

Step 3₅ Considerations

1. Who or what is the God of your understanding?

2. Do you have the gift of desperation to improve your life?

3. Is there anything or anyone who might interfere with your ability to follow good orderly direction?

4. What does it mean to you to "turn your will over?" How will you do that?

5. What does it mean to you to turn your life over? How will you do that?

Step 4_s

*Took a searching inventory of our
assets, talents and capabilities.*

Waking up after years of numbing addictive behavior can be overwhelming. That is precisely why the Sequel is recommended for people who have been in recovery for two years or more. The first trip through the steps focused on unearthing those nasty secrets, shameful acts, character defects and shortcomings. Most people taking an inventory in sobriety recognize that many of the wrongs done under the influence of addictive behavior were purely a byproduct of the addiction. For example: Few would steal from a parent or company if there were no need to support a gambling, shopping, or drug habit. There is usually no impulse to steal when we manage our own lives. In recovery we learn to be honest and open. The backs of many sobriety coins are imprinted with the motto, "To thine own self be true." In doing the 4th step, we review times when we may not have been honest. Again, most will discover their dishonesty was directly related to their addiction. Compulsive eaters deny stopping for fast food; drinkers say they have only had two when the true count is in the double digits and workaholics say they could not sleep when in reality they were drinking coffee to stay up working. The addict will end up lying about something to someone in order to avoid confrontation so addictive disorders can persist. These are just two of the many character defects common to all addictions; shortcomings which must be addressed before the individual is capable of truly evaluating his or her attributes. Having taken a searching and fearless moral inventory and continuing on with the remaining 8 steps, most recovering people are able to let go of the past. Once they have thoroughly completed the 12 steps, they will not be the same people they were in active addiction. The question then is, "How to discover who we are once we are sober?"

Sequel Step 4 asks you to begin identifying who you are as a recovering person. The addictive behaviors and substances which once impacted every aspect of our lives are no longer there. Once the character defects are removed, what are our attributes? We are free to be who we want to be and do what we want to do. For a brave few, this is a wonderful, exhilarating realization; for many it is overwhelming, frightening, and confusing. If you enter recovery with a clear sense of your sober self; certain of your goals for the future; grab the baton and run! Perhaps it is not imperative for you to labor through 4_S but still it will be helpful to jot down your assets, talents and capabilities. If you are like many people entering recovery, uncertain about who you are and what you want for your life in sobriety, forge on. Step 4_S asks that you list your resources, skills and abilities.

Start with your assets. What resources do you have? Think basics. Do you have a home? A car? If so, you are ahead of many newly recovering addicts. If you have been clean and sober for two years or more, you may have already begun to build assets. Approach this step with an attitude of gratitude. You should recognize that, although you may see many of these assets as common place, they are not for many in the world. Are you healthy? If so, you have the most important asset: life. Initially, the road to happy destiny may seem incredibly long and steep but, with continued recovery and a few basic resources, almost anything is possible.

Education is an asset. It is a foundation upon which more education may be built. Addiction may have thwarted even the brightest individual from completing high school. Recovery provides the clarity of mind required to return to and complete your formal education. If you already have a high school diploma you are qualified for many jobs, a college diploma perhaps qualifies you for even more. These are strengths that can be used to develop a more satisfying life.

Assets also include family and friends. Family members may provide direct financial support or they may offer housing, paving the way to obtain more education or training. Friends may offer to share living space, provide assistance with childcare, or tutoring for exams. Many times the greatest resource offered by friends and family is the enthusiastic encouragement we receive as we emerge from addiction into recovery. Look to the winners in the 12-step rooms, those people who have continued to improve their lives in recovery. They can share their experience, strength and hope evidencing the vast possibilities that enable us to flourish in our recovery.

Take care not to overlook the assets you may not like but which have considerable value. For example, if you are a car mechanic but tired of turning a wrench, those skills can be used to meet expenses while you develop new talents to change careers. If you are a practicing physician tired of patient care, consider how your degree and experience might be an asset moving into education, practice management or medical equipment sales. A stay-at-home parent may itch to return to the workplace but consider offering in-home childcare until new skills can be developed. As you inventory your assets, begin with all the talents you currently manifest. Our skills and talents are resources. If we review our life experience we begin to identify ingredients that can be used to make a new future. What are your specific talents? Can you cook well? Do you have mechanical ability? Are you creative? Each one of us has talents.

Looking back you may say you had a talent for getting into trouble; hopefully that is changing in sobriety. But if you had a talent for "getting into trouble;" what type of trouble was it? Consider the young man with a "talent" for getting speeding tickets. If his tickets are only for speeding and not for other violations, he must really be a good driver. Someone who speeds frequently and does not have accidents clearly knows how to handle a car. So driving is a talent that can be put on the list to help develop new opportunities in sobriety. Perhaps you have a history of challenging authority or being "insubordinate" by questioning company policy. Addicts tend to be impulsive during the disease process, perhaps your talent for getting in trouble with higher-ups had more to do with your timing than your ideas. Constructive criticism offered with possible solutions may now earn positive recognition. The point is, not everything identified as "bad" in one context is bad in another. After identifying the problems you had during your using days, consider strengths that may be hidden under "trouble."

Other skills and talents are more commonly recognized and may be easy to list. Musical skill, the ability to differentiate sounds, to recall lyrics, or to play an instrument are all talents that can be developed. Mechanical ability has application to a wide variety of vocations and hobbies. Technical abilities are in demand in every industry and in most homes of the 21st century. Organizational ability is a much needed skill for many careers; if you are good at organizing, put it on top of the list. The ability to organize a garage or kitchen may foretell the ability to administer a courthouse or manage a business. Do not rule out any of your talents or skills when doing 4_s, write them all down. As you write you may note things that you think you would be good at but have not had the opportunity to develop your skills in those areas. These are your capabilities.

Capabilities are skills that have yet to be developed. Anyone with basic intelligence and reasonably good health has many un-mined capabilities. We are capable of almost anything. Several years ago, I met a woman who was taking 28 different medications, most related to, or because of, psychological problems. She had the capability of getting off all but two of those medications, and she did. That would never have happened if she had not listed the ability to get off her medication as one of her capabilities. That woman went on to lose 80 pounds, complete marathons, get a college degree and enter nursing school. At the beginning of her recovery, no one would have anticipated her capabilities. Every recovering addict has already proven they have the capability of discontinuing addictive behavior. That is a formidable task, often more difficult than any others that might be attempted. In recovery we have the capability of maintaining a job, being a friend, and developing skills and talents. We have new capacities to improve our lives. Make a list of your capabilities; identify those potential resources that might evolve into talents to enhance your life.

Here are a few examples of what others have done:

Steve began his recovery from inside a locked psychiatric facility. He had been a compulsive athlete, swimming almost 4 hours every day. He smoked marijuana often and drank whenever he could. Steve failed out of one prestigious university and was about to fail out of a second when his drug use triggered a Bipolar Disorder, landing him in a psychiatric hospital. After being medically stabilized, Steve began working a 12-step program. During his first two years of recovery he attended meetings daily and therapy weekly. As he approached his second anniversary and was about to graduate with a BA in journalism, he took stock of his assets and talents. He had experienced a couple false starts in business management and coaching, but finally he completed a 4_s^{th} step and set a new path. Steve put together his people skills, business knowledge, family ties and financial resources. He partnered with his father and developed a successful mortgage business at a time when many similar businesses were failing. Steve relied on his experience competing in sports to keep him in the game of competing in business. Today he is happily married, owns his own home and has a successful career.

Candy came from an entirely different set of circumstances and conditions. She entered recovery after a cold-turkey withdrawal in county jail. A mother of two teenage sons, she knew she had to stay clean. After jail, she started attending NA meetings and working the 12 steps. Eventually she enrolled in college and then graduate school. Ultimately, she applied for licensure as a Professional Counselor. Today she has a successful private practice focused on helping others recover from addiction. Candy evaluated her skills and talents. She knew she wanted to help people, especially addicts. She was not sure she had a talent for school, but she knew she had the capacity. She worked hard and developed new assets, college degrees, to enable her to establish a new career.

Roger entered recovery from the back of a patrol car after being arrested for possession of pain medication and a firearm. Roger had been working to complete a degree in social work. A brief stint in jail interrupted his education, enabling him to complete the 12 steps and begin the sequel. As he evaluated his talents and assets, Roger realized that he had no interest in social work. What Roger loved was cars. In fact, there was little Roger did not know about cars. In short order, he changed his career path, went to work for an automotive parts distributor and began working his way up the corporate ladder. No longer struggling with a sense of inadequacy in academia, he was catapulted into a position where he could excel. His success resulted in a newfound sense of self-esteem and self-worth which, in turn, enabled him to return to dating.

Beatrice, on the other hand, had no interest in education. She had dropped out of high school in 11th grade, weakened by anorexia and unable to pass her classes. She had lived with a series of boyfriends until age 25 when she first walked into a 12-step meeting. Over the next several years she managed to stabilize her weight and complete the steps. She worked as a Sous Chef and later ran a kitchen for a prestigious private college. Even with the free tuition offered by her employer, Bea had no interest in formal education. Bea's talent was focused on food; she could cook and present meals that were on par with elite chefs. When it came time for Bea to do 4_s, it was evident that her best talent was cooking. Today Bea owns a very successful restaurant.

These are but a few of the many success stories of people who took an inventory of their assets, talents and capabilities to help guide them in their continued recovery. Most had the assistance of a sponsor, career coach or therapist along the way. Another set of eyes and ears is always beneficial to ensure you do not miss something. It is recommended that once you take your inventory, you share it with another person.

Step 4$_s$ Considerations

1. How are you different today from before?

2. Develop a gratitude list of things recovered, discovered or lost that prepare you for a new life in recovery.

3. Are you proud of your talents?

4. Are you comfortable letting others know you have assets?

5. How can you manifest your skills to help yourself and others?

Step 5₅

Admitted to God, to ourselves and another human being the exact nature of our potential as sober individuals.

The only reason you are able to read this book is because I admitted to God, to myself and to a slew of other beings the exact nature of my potential to write about this subject. At first it did not seem to make any difference but, as I worked with the ideas, shared them at meetings and passed out copies of the Sequel Steps, people started asking about the book. A couple recovery bookstores wanted to stock it and friends in recovery wanted to read it. Finally it became an embarrassment that it was not done and the push was on. Knowing I could write was not enough. Admitting my potential only to family members was not very effective either. I was able to ignore or placate them by pointing out how hard I was working in other areas of my life (and theirs). Approximately a year before the book was submitted for publication, I began admitting my potential to God and asked for support and guidance. Be careful what you pray for! Troops arrived and at every corner it seemed someone was asking about my progress or urging me forward. It became imperative to finish the project. I shifted from knowing I *could* do it to believing I would do it.

To complete the 5th step in the sequel (5_s) you must adopt the attitude of the optimist. A skeptic lives a life of doubt, questioning things. "I'll believe it when I see it." The optimist affirms, "I'll see it when I believe it." You must be willing to believe continued growth is possible. This should be easy if you have already done the 12 steps. Recovery brings many changes. If there is one thing we do know, we know we can change. Why limit our vision?

Throughout history, prophets, world leaders, self-help authors, and religious writers have extolled man's ability to adapt and progress. All educational systems make the assumption that people can learn new things. Freudian psychologists once believed that the individual's personality and approach to life were essentially set by age 5. We now see octogenarians going to college, finishing marathons, and embarking on new endeavors. We only stop growing if we choose to or if we die. If you are reading this book, you are not dead and you probably want to keep growing. Bravo! Let's get to it. But how?

Start with **believing**. Believe you can grow. Believe you can stay abstinent. Believe you can do almost anything that you can envision and start visioning. Begin by thinking about what you would like most to do. Fantasize what your ideal life would look like. How would you spend your days? Painting masterpieces or painting houses? Cooking wonderful meals for your family or running a chain of restaurants? Performing surgery or delivering Meals on Wheels?

Many years ago I counseled a young man who had been addicted to heroin and had recently detoxed off methadone. He was an active member of Narcotics Anonymous, dedicating many hours each week to the local Helpline. Darius was committed to recovery, his and others'. All went well until his boss, a physician, asked him to inventory the narcotics cabinet. Darius began to romance the drug. He decided to quit the job to protect his recovery. It was time, he reasoned, to pursue his dreams. He believed he could do more with his life, but had little training or experience. Darius worked the 3rd Step, he turned his will and his job opportunities over to God. The only jobs immediately available were with a temp agency. One week, the only job available was an entry level position in optical manufacturing. Needing to work, he took that job. Within five years he was the Director of Manufacturing. The company's tuition reimbursement program allowed him to take engineering courses and improve his skills. He never completed a degree. He left the company, went to other companies, took jobs that he did not enjoy to gain experience, took jobs that he thought he would enjoy but did not, and gradually developed an impressive professional resume. With each job success or disappointment, he assessed what new skills or insights he had to offer the next employer. Today, Darius works from home as part of a global technical development team. He tells others, "It's a lot of fun – I love my job. It's like a hobby." Darius attributes his success to working the steps. He worked the first 12 to protect his recovery and then applied the principles of the Sequel to maximize his potential. Darius was passionate about developing his assets, talents and capabilities to their fullest potential.

If you have a passion, follow it! Mihaly Csikszentmihalyi, the author of *Flow: The Psychology of Optimal Experience*, identifies optimal experience as "being in the flow." He describes this state as one that fully absorbs the individual. When you are optimally experiencing the world you are fully engaged, energized and involved in the activity at hand. In the midst of editing this chapter, a young man engaged the author in a conversation about his future career. A third year law student, Barnard was working as a paralegal in a criminal law firm. We stood in the kitchen for nearly 30 minutes discussing issues related to substance abuse, felonies and misdemeanors. Barnard missed a pivotal play in a football game but did not stop to inquire, he was deep in conversation. Eventually I withdrew to return to my work, but Barnard was quick to suggest we continue the conversation at another time. Now it is noteworthy that there were at least 4 other law students and 2 J.D.'s visiting to watch the opening game, none of whom cared to discuss law over football. The difference is clear: Barnard is in the flow. He has chosen a career that optimizes his talents and is drawn to discuss his passion at every opportunity. In order to find those activities which will incite your passions, you must identify what has the most meaning in your life. When you find it, the doors will open or you will have the energy to create new doors.

It is a challenge for many people to determine exactly what they truly love to do. To begin, I suggest a type of dowsing. For those unfamiliar with the term, dowsing is a type of divination. A technique used to find hidden resources, historically to find water, minerals or gems. If one can find precious minerals using the technique, it should be possible to use a similar process to find hidden skills. But first let us explore how dowsers find water or minerals. Typically they use a divining rod. The traditional divining rod is a Y- or L- shaped branch. The rod is loosely held as the dowser moves slowly over the land. Reportedly, the branch bends or twitches when near the desired substance. The dowser waits for the slightest twitch in the rod to signify the presence of life-giving water or precious metals.

To "divine" your optimal path, set out over your land - move out in your social network, community or throughout the world. Investigate careers, look at different workplace settings, evaluate educational programs and wait for a twitch. A twitch? Yes, as you imagine all things possible, what draws you specifically toward it? What career brings you immediately to the computer to research training opportunities? Do you marvel at the fact someone gets paid to be a park ranger? Do you fantasize about working on Wall Street? What section do you go to first in the bookstore? What papers did you write before they were due in college? Is there a section of the craft or home improvement store that seems to have a magnetic field pulling you in every time you get close? Watch what interests you, pay attention. Those "twitches" manifest as enthusiasm, energy, and excitement. When you find the best path it can be orgasmic; there will be no doubt when you find your bliss.[14]

Following your bliss may challenge the family or social expectation that you "should" do something else. Suppose great granddad started a manufacturing company and the entire family works in the business. Throughout your childhood, you worked in the factory and helped in the retail stores. In college, you studied organizational psychology so you could help run the business. But you hate the industry and do not particularly want to spend every work day with your Dad and Uncles. You find a nonprofit dedicated to helping disabled children and you volunteer every waking moment with that organization. At work, you are lethargic but after work, while helping kids, you are energized. Then one day, the Board of Directors of the nonprofit asks if you would be willing to replace the retiring CEO and manage the expansion of the agency. What to do? Risk staying with the family business with the possibility of returning to alcohol to sedate the frustration? Many people face significant pressure to follow in a parent's footsteps without consideration for their best capabilities. Caving under these pressures can lead one to failure in following their bliss. The mentally, physically and spiritually fit choice is to pursue your passions.

Women often feel obliged to limit their options due to gender stereotypes. Some cultures have strict limitations on the roles women may take in society. Until the mid-70's, many American and European women encountered glass ceilings which limited their advancement in business and industry. A few remarkable women pushed past convention and followed their dreams. Amelia Earhart and Madame Curie were women who changed mankind pursuing their passions. Unfortunately, for every one person who follows their bliss, there are hundreds that do not. How many great performers, scientists, artists, etc. have been lost when loved ones admonished them to "major in a subject that will provide a job and a good income"?

The main message is: Do what you love! When you achieve your flow, you will be doing something you are passionate about. If you are passionate, you will be energized by your work. If you are energized, you will be engaged. If you are engaged, you will stick with it and learn. If you learn all there is to learn, you will be successful. If you are successful, people will reward you. For performers, the currency of success may be audience approval rather than financial reward. Parents who stay home to rear their children benefit daily as they watch the children grow and learn. Love to teach? Educators are typically underpaid but receive many additional benefits that provide stability as well as a satisfying life. If you have an entrepreneurial spirit your reward will most likely be financial. What is important to recognize is that if you love what you are doing, you will learn to do it well and be rewarded in meaningful ways. The best part of all is that if you are doing what you love, the work itself is sufficiently rewarding.

To follow your bliss, it is necessary to admit to God, yourself and another human being the exact nature of your potential as a sober individual. If a tree falls in the forest and no one hears it, does it make a noise? Of course, but does anyone notice? Of course not! If you do not share your gifts, goals and plans with someone else, they remain dreams. Admitting to another human being the exact nature of your potential virtually seals the deal. You are more likely to do something if you have told someone else you will do it. Think about how many things you do solely because you have admitted your intention to another human being: Yes, I will attend your graduation. I will be in to work this Saturday. I am going back to college. Monday is laundry day. Sure, I will make your favorite meal for dinner. Meet you at the gym. The list can go on endlessly. We are social beings; we like to share what we do with others. It should come as no surprise then that by admitting to God, to yourself and another human being the exact nature of your potential, you are much more likely to move forward.

Sharing goals is particularly necessary for those most ravaged by addiction. There is a woman I have known for 4 years who still looks every bit like a street person. If you were to encounter her in almost any environment, you would use caution speaking with her. You might wonder if she is homeless, mentally ill or mentally deficient. In reality she is brilliant, without a doubt intellectually gifted. Yes, she has mental health issues, but those are being resolved as she achieves a stable recovery. She is not homeless, she lives in a nice apartment on the water. No one would expect Elesia would be capable of going to college and entering a human service profession, but that is exactly what she plans to do. She has already taken the placement exams and scored very well. By telling others she has the intention of getting her college education she has made a commitment to move forward.

Recently I attended a workshop at a nationally renowned treatment center for substance abuse. While there, I was impressed by the knowledge and capability of a man who ran two of the units. Later, I discovered that he began his employment at the center working in the kitchen. When first hired he was newly sober, had few skills and had not graduated from high school. Fifteen years later, he had finished college, had two Master's degrees and was working on a PhD. There is no doubt he told people what his plans were. As he shared his story, he received continued support and encouragement along the way. By sharing with others, asking for help, and having faith, the guy who once took out the trash became an administrator at the facility.

We have to tell people what we intend to do. When we tell people, we let the cat out of the bag. We acknowledge that we can do and be more than what we are currently doing or being. By telling ourselves, we can set up a craving, a compelling urge to get, do or be something. Consider your earlier experiences with cravings. Once you admitted you wanted another pint of ice cream, horse race, bag of dope, college degree, etc., that thought preoccupied your mind until you followed through and got what you wanted. In recovery we learn to replace bad compulsions with good ones. Step 5ₛ enhances recovery by providing something positive to crave.

Step 5$_s$ Considerations

1. Do you truly believe you will change your life?

2. Why do you want to change your life?

3. If you could do anything in the world, what would it be? Can you do it? Why or why not?

4. Do you deserve to be happy?

5. Is it okay to succeed? Would it be okay to be more successful than you are today?

Step 6$_S$

Identified our characteristics, skills and talents that can now be put to good use.

As you embark on this part of the journey to optimize wellness, it will be helpful to re-visit your 4$_S$ inventory. 4$_S$ identifies your assets, talents and capabilities. Much like the founders of AA used different words to identify defects, here I employ slightly different terminology to further identify assets. Peeking ahead to 7$_S$, you will note that we are going to ask God to support and guide our future development. Listing our characteristics, skills and talents helps define that direction.

Addictive disease usually creates situations and compulsions that demand we deviate from our true selves. Waking up in recovery can be traumatic. Many years of addiction may result in a negative, self-denigrating attitude. We begin recovery running away from addiction. Our direction is defined by avoidance. We avoid defects of character and shortcomings as well as past people, places and things. To continue growing, it is imperative that we let go of that past. Effective working of the 12 steps may remove our sense of shame and guilt, but it does not replace the old self-concept with a new one. The sequel, Step 6$_S$ asks you to look at the other side of the coin, to take ownership of your positive qualities.

Here are some definitions that might help you identify those attributes:

Characteristics

Characteristics are enduring patterns of psychological function. In 1921 Carl Jung provided a lexicon for psychological types. His model has been the basis for modern typologies of personality.[15] The dimensions described in his book *Psychological Types* (Jung, 1921) provide a useful structure to begin identifying your greatest strengths.

Extraversion versus introversion

Dr. Jung identified two primary styles of expressing oneself in the world, extraversion and introversion. His concepts go far beyond the common use of the terms extravert and introvert. Being extraverted or introverted are not synonymous with being the life of the party or a wall flower. These terms reflect how you are energized. Everyone falls somewhere on the continuum; there are few who are exclusively introverted or extraverted. In order to obtain optimal satisfaction, it is essential that your life is structured to accommodate your preferences for interacting with others

An extravert must interact with others to sustain vital energy and enthusiasm for life. In contrast, the introvert must have time alone to reflect and re-energize. It has been said that extraverts act and introverts think. This does not mean introverts do not act and extraverts do not think. It means that shared activity excites and energizes an extravert while quiet time to think energizes an introvert. Since these dimensions identify how social interaction can either fuel or exhaust motivation, we must honor our preferred style if we wish to maximally succeed.

Perhaps you already know whether you are introverted or extraverted. If not, answering a few simple questions should help you decide.

- When invited to a party, do you prefer to go late and leave early or do you arrive early and leave late?

- On a day off, do you relish the free time to do just what you want to do, spending most of that time alone? Or do you call all your friends, find out where the action is, and stay as busy as possible?

- During family or group events, do you find a way to excuse yourself for some private time or do you keep the activities going?

- After being with people, even people you love and enjoy, do you feel worn out? Or do you leave social events enthusiastic and looking for more people to do things with?

If you answered "yes" to the first of each of the above question pairs, you are definitely an introvert. This is not a character defect as some might suggest[16], it is your style of interacting with the world. Time alone re-energizes an introvert. If you answered "no" to the first of each of the above questions and "yes" to the second, you are definitely an extravert. An extravert who does not want the party to end is not suffering from immaturity; his or her extraverted nature is fueled by social interaction.

It is important for you to evaluate how much alone time you need and how much social interaction you need. If you are strongly extraverted, it would be unwise to pursue a vocation or avocation that demands many hours of solitary work. Similarly, it would also be unwise to pursue activities that require constant social interaction if you are strongly introverted. Once you identify yourself along the extraverted/introverted continuum, you can plan your time with others accordingly. You can move forward in your recovery understanding why you prefer to lead the group or to follow. When with others you can bask in the energy that feeds your extraverted soul. In contrast, if you are an introvert, you will be cognizant that you will need time alone to recharge.

Sensation versus intuition

Sensing and intuiting are perceiving functions; they represent characteristic styles of seeing the world. When you evaluate the world, do you rely almost exclusively on information that can be sensed? If so, your style is to operate within the concrete world, focusing on what can be seen, touched, or proven. You will be more satisfied with activities that are "hands on," allowing you to manipulate tangible things rather than ideas. You will want the facts, and just the facts. If you are sensation dominant, you will do best in occupations and hobbies that are data or object based, rather than theory or concept based. Sensing types delight in gathering information, taking pictures, and uncovering the details of personal experience. Sensing individuals make great craftsmen, dentists, and chefs.

Intuition based individuals are less inclined to gather concrete data or remember details. They operate in the abstract, distilling ideas and relating events. Individuals who are intuition based will be reading this book to get the concepts, and may not ever remember the steps. Those guided by intuition are more likely to respond to a hunch. They tend to engage in activities just for the experience. Intuitive types make great childcare workers, psychologists and politicians.

If, as you read these descriptors, you find yourself critical of one mode or another, that is a good indication that you are the opposite of that mode. For example, if you think it is irresponsible for people to act on a whim or take action based on an "intuitive sense" without supportive data, you are definitely a sensing type. On the other hand, if you become frustrated when others do exhaustive internet searches before making a decision, you are probably an intuitive type. Types refer to what the individual prefers. Trust your instincts, what feels right or logically makes sense, when determining which type best fits your dominant style.

Thinking versus Feeling

These are the judging functions. They identify your preferred style for making decisions about the world. The sensing/intuition continuum identifies how you gather information; the thinking/feeling continuum identifies how you process that information.

Are you a thinker? Do you evaluate all the information at hand? Are you constantly turning something over in your mind? Does debate excite you? Do you rely on past experience to evaluate future probability? When making a decision are you generally detached and logical? Thinkers rely on objective, logical processing of experience and perception. They make great judges. Judges are required to make decisions based on fact, reason and law. There is little opportunity to consider feelings when making a judicial decision.

Perhaps, instead, you are a feeler. Feelers are guided by an understanding and concern for how a decision will seem to others. Individuals who are dominant in the feeling mode make decisions based on the greatest good for the greatest number of people, even when that decision may not be the most economical or logical. Feelers cry when watching sad movies. They rejoice when the underdog pulls ahead. They have great capacity for empathy. Feelers often advocate for social policy legislation. They excel in human service positions.

As indicated above, if you find yourself critical of one modality and supportive of the other, it identifies your preferred style. If you are a feeling type, it will be very difficult for you to move into a career or activity that requires strict adherence to rules and guidelines. Conversely, if you are a thinking type, it will drive you crazy to participate in activities or work for organizations that do not have a defined structure.

For the purpose of Step 6ₛ, it is not critical that you determine your personality type. However, it may be helpful to understand how these characteristics influence what you will enjoy most. The Sequel is designed to maximize your happiness and success. Examining your personality type helps point you in the direction of the goals and activities you are most likely to enjoy. It is also wise to evaluate your skill set. By determining what skills you already have, you can increase the likelihood of success moving forward.

Skills

Our skills serve as a jumping off point; they do not need to define or limit us. By developing a list of abilities you already have, you establish a baseline of current resources. The term "skills" refers to the capacity to complete tasks with relative ease. Looking back on years of addictive behavior you may feel as though you have few capabilities, but that is seldom the case. I have met many former drug dealers who have exquisite skills at managing money and negotiation. A recovered anorexic may have more skills for diet management than many dieticians. Former gamblers have great skill at maintaining focus when facing seeming disaster. Workaholics tend to be great at multi-tasking. No matter how severe your addiction may have been, you got out alive so you have the capability to survive.

Start with your addiction history. Look back, certainly you developed skills along the way although they may not be immediately apparent. Some skills will be specific to one environment or situation, but others may generalize leading to many new opportunities.

Specific skills

If you have had any paying or non-paying job for several years, you most likely developed skills related to that work. Professionals reading this will have a ready list of skills from their former or current career. Put these skills on a list so you can appreciate what you have already learned. Be careful not to pigeonhole yourself into one professional identity. In recovery, you may discover many new activities to pursue. For those of you without a specific career, do not worry. Skills are developed in even the most basic jobs and activities. For example, when a mom volunteers to help in her child's classroom she develops many skills from interacting with the school administration and working with children. A restaurant server often has good customer relations skills. Custodians typically have good organizational skills; they can stay on task and get work projects done. Salespeople have good conversational skills and the ability to influence others. A coach knows how to motivate people. "Just a laborer?" Most laborers exhibit great strength and resilience. Imagine the fortitude of the individuals who are willing to work in the hot Florida sun despite being up to the wee hours getting high. Even the youngest of recovering people may find a skill set in the ability they had in avoiding detection by teachers and parents. One of the most skillful addicts I have ever encountered stole a great deal of money from me, along with my identity. The way she manipulated funds to mask her embezzlement revealed great skill in both bookkeeping and presenting a proper public image. Do not dismiss your past; whatever you have done, a skill set can be found.

If you have difficulty developing a list of your specific skills, talk with friends and family members. Ask them what they notice about you, what skills they see. If you have a resume, review it, listing the tasks you did in each job. The task list will give you insight into what skills you developed for that job. Once this list is done, consider the general skills most people have and recognize those capabilities in you as well.

General skills

These are the skills that are most often overlooked. The capabilities most of us take for granted. Can you use a keyboard? Search the internet? Do you use online banking or manage a household budget? Can you cook a meal and finish each item at the same time? When there is a family crisis, can you respond calmly? If something breaks are you usually able to fix it? If you are not able to fix it, can you easily access another resource? Do you have good math skills? Are you comfortable talking on the phone?

General skills are the reading, writing and arithmetic elements in day-to-day life. If you can make a grocery list, buy everything on the list, bring it home, put it away and later use some of those items to make a meal, there is evidence of many general skills. You can assess what is needed in a situation (stock the pantry), follow directions (complete the list), finish a task (bring the items home), manage space and organize (put things away), and plan an event (prepare a meal). Take some time and evaluate these hidden skills and add them to your list.

Talents

Talents represent those special skills and abilities that set you apart from others, things you can uniquely do. We most often think of talents in terms of performance, someone having great musical or artistic talent. But talents can be found in many aspects of day-to-day life.

Problem solving is a talent. Understanding people is a talent. Are you usually able to figure out how something works and how to fix it? Do you have a specific aptitude that makes certain types of activities easy for you? Do you understand numbers? Can you manage a group easily? Do you have a talent for picking up new information and applying it? If you do not have a long list of skills that have already been developed, you may be like Mary. Mary proudly told me that she had never taken a job she knew how to do. She had a talent for learning and applying new information. When I met her she had just released the reigns of a nonprofit organization she had developed to support a local performing arts center. Previously, she had run her husband's accounting firm, worked in hospital administration and owned a retail clothing store. Mary never finished college, but she had many talents, including the ability to market her skills.

Consider the talents needed to perpetuate addictive behavior. Many eating disordered individuals have great talent at avoiding detection when binging or purging. Gamblers typically have great talent at manipulating money, and often at manipulating people into believing they are a good credit risk. Workaholics have great talent at justifying their inability to participate in recreational activities. Drug addicts often develop great talent at circumventing rules and laws. This is not to suggest that deception is beneficial. Rather it is to examine the talents developed to perpetuate addictive behavior and then use those talents for positive pursuits in recovery.

Again, it may be beneficial to ask others what they perceive your talents to be. A parent or partner may quip, "You have a talent for getting out of trouble." Or you may hear, "You're our social organizer." Perhaps someone will lament the fact that your artistic or performance talent was never developed. Listen to the responses you get and add those that seem valid to your list of talents.

If you have taken time with 6$_S$, you will have a fairly lengthy list. Your characteristics, skills and talents may be disparate, with no clear focus, or they may neatly point you in a logical direction to improve your life. Whatever the case, it is now time to ask for help. That is the point of Step 7$_S$.

Step 6$_s$ Considerations

1. Are you an introvert or an extravert? How will that impact your life choices?

2. What is your preferred decision making style? Do you like making decisions?

3. Do you prefer hands-on, concrete activities or more conceptual, intellectual activities?

4. List the talents you enjoy the most.

5. Identify the skills you wish to develop further.

Step 7₅

*Humbly asked God to guide and
support our future development.*

As you begin Step 7_S, it is time once more to let go of your preconceived notions of what the future holds. 3_S asks you to turn your will and your life over. 4_S through 6_S help define your strengths and capabilities. When you work 7_S, you commit to personal growth. By asking a power greater than yourself to guide and support your future, you open the door for more possibilities than you might imagine. This is a joint effort. God can move mountains, but you need to bring a shovel. Working Step 7_S requires you to grab the shovel and ask for help.

Many people question how they can know what God's will for them is. In turning their lives and their wills over to the care of God, they wonder how they will know they are being cared for and guided. My general recommendation is to let go and follow **good orderly direction**. Do the next right thing. Follow the path until there is a roadblock. If you cannot find a way to circumnavigate a barrier, move in a direction that is unobstructed. God writes straight using crooked lines. Sometimes a detour leads straight to your greatest reward. Recovery becomes an exciting adventure when you are moving forward toward new accomplishments. One note of caution: Whether you are moving mountains or climbing them, it is best to move gradually and with conscious intention.

Of course we do not literally move mountains; it is a metaphor from the Christian Bible. Matthew 17:20 reads, "He [Jesus] replied, 'Because you have so little faith. I tell you the truth, if you have faith as small as a mustard seed, you can say to this mountain, 'Move from here to there' and it will move. Nothing will be impossible for you.'" (The Holy Bible, New International Version, 2011) This was the response Jesus gave to his disciples when asked how he could do things others could not. The message is: if you believe you can do something, it can be done. This is a critical concept for anyone challenging themselves to escape the cycle of addiction. Resilience, the ability to recover from misfortune, rests on a "can do" attitude. To succeed you need faith, confidence that you can and will improve your life (possibly beyond your wildest dreams). Of course we all have some limits. Most people, however, over-estimate their limits and under-estimate their capabilities. It is far more limiting to believe you cannot do something that is possible than it is to believe you can do something that is not possible. Even if you attempt the impossible and fail, you will succeed in identifying one option that is not possible! Thomas Edison is often quoted as saying that he did not fail to create a light bulb 10,000 times, but found 10,000 ways not to make a light bulb. Through perseverance, Edison found a way to make a light bulb and improved lives all over the world.

Throughout history, the people who have made the greatest difference in the world have shared the traits of resilience and determination to move forward. Nelson Mandela held firm to his political beliefs for over 25 years in prison. Upon his release, he continued his life work. He was elected President of the African National Congress and received the Nobel Peace Prize. In his 80's, he retired from political office. He continued to work, however, raising funds to help Africa's poor and consulting with world leaders to find solutions for global problems. On a less public, but equally remarkable scale, Tom I. first attended AA in the Michigan State Penitentiary. He tells a story of waking up in jail only to discover that he had killed two people while driving in a blackout. He was suicidal and filled with self-hate. According to his story, he had no real interest in attending meetings or being released. In an AA room of 300 felons, he learned about the disease of alcoholism and began his recovery. After he was paroled, he moved to North Carolina and volunteered to bring meetings into the State Prison. When the State Prison system wanted to start a rehabilitation program, they approached Tom and offered him a job. He retired 39 years later after serving in many capacities, including warden. Nelson Mandela and Tom I. share two important traits: their belief in a power greater than themselves and a willingness to accept the help and support of others. The resultant changes in their lives improved the world around them.

John F. Kennedy identified change as "the law of life." He cautioned that those who look only to the past or present will miss the future (Kennedy, 1963). If we do not grow in recovery, we become stagnant. Abstinence must be our primary goal early in sobriety. Going to meetings, working the steps, turning it over, asking for help, and avoiding triggers to relapse maintains our recovery. We do the same thing over and over again and get the same positive result. We become available to do more and be more. The Sequel Steps guide us into the future using the same principles that allowed us to escape the past.

It is risky to take on any major journey without a map or directions. So in 7_s, we humbly ask for support and guidance. The support can be emotional, financial, spiritual or all three. Support relates to additional help, something you can seek out when you need assistance. It is easy to see how we rely on support from people and institutions around us.

Our friends and families (of origin or choice) support us emotionally. We might also consult a career counselor or life coach to help us move past our 6_S list. Financially, we may support ourselves by finding paid work or by applying for grants, public assistance or loans to help us reach a goal. Spiritually, we pray for help from the God of our understanding and meditate to access the spirit within.

Our inner voice speaks to us through the "twitches" discussed in Chapter 5 and in a variety of other ways. Often, it is sufficient to approach life with a mindfulness that allows you to see the possibilities around you. When the path is unclear, humbly ask for guidance and support then wait, remaining observant. Sleep on it. You should not overlook the power of the unconscious mind to distill information and provide new ideas. When we "sleep on something", we consider the options, taking time to evaluate what is happening. When we wake up in the morning, we have a clearer sense as to what is best for us. Sometimes, "sleeping on it" provides rather dramatic information that communicates what is in our best (or worst) interest. This information often comes through dreams and dream imagery.

Dreams are believed to symbolize information being processed by the unconscious mind. This may be true of both night-dreams and day-dreams. Day-dreams are generally easier to interpret. When we day-dream, we are consciously thinking about something we would like to do or experience. These dreams usually portray our deepest hopes and aspirations. Night-dreams are sometimes cluttered with day residue, images and emotions of things we experienced the day before. Night-dreams tend to be more symbolic and difficult to interpret. In both day-dreams and night-dreams, the emotions we experience often reveal how we are feeling about the dream content. For example: If you day-dream about returning to college, and envisioning yourself in the library studying gets you excited, it is a good indicator that you are ready to return to school. If, on the other hand, you see yourself in the library and feel stressed, it is a good sign that you should not attempt a return to school at this time.

Ellie's dreams transformed her future. Initially, it was her intent to follow in her parents' footsteps by moving into one of the family real estate investment companies. She was majoring in business at an elite private college. As Ellie began her upper level management classes, her attention was drawn to volunteering in social service projects. She kept day-dreaming about new ideas to help children. At night, the dreams Ellie remembered were all about children. She dreamt of being at Disney World on the "It's a Small, Small World" ride. She dreamt of coaching tennis at a children's after-school program. And she dreamt of student teaching in an elementary school. It was the last of these dreams that cued her to consider an alternate career. Ellie changed her major, completed her degree, and went on to teach elementary school. She frequently worked 14 hour days but never complained; she loved the children and loved what she was doing.

Like Ellie, Joe started out following in his father's footsteps, working long hours at the family-owned restaurant. After being robbed one night, just outside the restaurant, he began to have nightmares about being hurt during work. At first he discounted the night-dreams as posttraumatic material. Soon, however, new images replaced the old ones. In these images, Joe was in a building that resembled the diner but there was music and a much younger clientele. He was sitting with a group of his friends watching sports. One afternoon, when business was particularly slow, Joe kept imagining the restaurant as it looked in his dream. He day-dreamed of transforming the space and envisioned a totally new concept. He followed his dreams and, within a year's time, transformed the outdated diner, which catered to local retirees, into a thriving hotspot for young professionals.

It is important to listen to your inner voice, the part of you which speaks to what you love in life. This is not selfish; this is a self-*centered* practice of respecting your Self. Many studies on human happiness and personal success stress the importance of becoming aware of what is important to you as an individual and following those personal passions. Watch for those twitches, small changes in your perspective or random ideas that pop up. If you have been asking for support and guidance, those quiet thoughts might be the guideposts you are looking for.

The world at large also provides immense possibility for assistance. If you have some idea of what you might like to do, it is wise to seek outside help. Direction may be found in institutions and through individuals specializing in mentoring and teaching. Directed support has a predetermined scope and usually an identified outcome, it is recommended if you are certain of what you wish to accomplish. If not, it is recommended that you seek others out to provide encouragement during the journey. General support may be found in religious institutions, self-help groups, professional organizations, and through psychotherapy. Perhaps one day, there even may be Sequel groups focused on maximizing wellness and success in recovery. Group support can affirm that change is necessary and growth is possible. When we humbly ask for guidance and support, we acknowledge that we do not have all the answers; we remain open to receive help from powers greater than ourselves.

Step 7ₛ Considerations

1. Which "shovels" have you picked up to move mountains in your path?

2. What past events hold you back?

3. What future events concern you?

4. Who are the members of your support network?

5. What dreams have you had lately?

Step 8_S

Made a list of goals and plans we envision for our future.

Pick up the shovel! By this point you may have lots of ideas about what you might like to do, and maybe even some ideas about how you might proceed. Now it is time to develop a concrete list of goals and the plans to reach them. Goals are necessary for personal growth, without them few would move forward. Most would remain stagnant and many would move backward. Goals are destinations. If we know where we are going, we can find the route to get there. If, however, we have no goal, we are likely to wander aimlessly. Consider the metaphor of driving. If you do not have a destination in mind when you get into your car, there is no reason to start the engine. If you do start the engine, it may only be to listen to the radio. The car will be operational, but will not go anywhere. If you decide to pull out of the parking space, you will quickly have to turn the wheel. But which way? If you have no destination, every corner and crossroad presents a quandary. Which way to turn? Before you have traveled a mile you may give up in frustration, returning to your original location because it is familiar.

Life, when we have not set a destination, can model driving. We move along in pinball fashion, bouncing off obstacles, occasionally falling in holes and ultimately ending back where we began. If we have a goal, it establishes a direction we can move toward. We can develop a route and make plans to get there. Goals can be broken into three types: immediate, short term and long term.

The immediate goals are things we can work on right away. Some basic immediate goals include improving health regimens, working on spiritual development, organizing work and leisure activity. You can begin working on these goals right now.

In matters of health, most of us can improve our diet, sleep and exercise routines. If you cringe at the word "diet", do not worry. I am not talking about losing weight; I am talking about improving nutrition. I do not recommend di-ets. Pronounce that word separating the syllables – di-eting implies dying. Many feel as if they are dying or could die on the diets that abound for weight loss. Food plans that are overly restrictive only set people up for failure. It is human nature to strive for independence and autonomy. It is difficult to feel happy, joyous and free if you are chained to a di-et. For the immediate moment, simply move in the direction of healthy eating. The guidelines are pretty easy: eat food that is minimally processed, decrease fats and sugars, and control portions. KISMIF! Keep it simple, make it fun.

Yes, eating can be fun and healthy too. If you approach menu planning with excitement instead of dread, you may discover you can enjoy food that is healthy. It may take a while, but it is well worth the effort. Start with foods you like. Do not eliminate any particular food or type of food. Even chocolate has been proven to have health benefits (Myklebust, 2010). Next, list options for breakfast, lunch, dinner and snacks. Identify foods that are healthy and can be eaten anytime (e.g. salad, fruit, and vegetables). Then begin to put together meal options. Below are some ideas to get started:

Breakfast:	Oatmeal with fruit, dried or fresh
	2 eggs and whole grain toast
	Yogurt and granola
	Assorted cereals with fiber and low in sugar
	Egg white omelets with veggies & low fat cheese
Lunch:	Salads with protein (chicken, shrimp, tuna, seeds & nuts)
	Tuna or chicken wraps
	6" veggie sub
	Dinner leftovers
Dinner:	Chicken, grilled or baked
	Fish
	Fajitas
	Vegetables lightly seasoned
	Green salad
	Whole grain pasta dishes
	Vegetarian lasagna
Snacks:	Fruit
	Pretzels & popcorn
	Yogurt
	PB & celery
	Low cal & fruit popsicles
	Dill or sour pickles

There are many low calorie, low glycemic index, healthy recipes online. If you approach meal planning as an adventure, you can find many new treats. If you prefer to eat out, check the restaurant's website before leaving home. Evaluate the selections and hone in on the healthiest choices before you sit down to order. You will discover that seemingly similar dishes have radically different nutritional values. One national Asian fast food chain offers salads that vary by over 400 calories and 1,000 mg of sodium. For others, nutritional information cannot be found. Be wary of those that do not offer nutritional information. Even salads may top 1500 calories, the total many people need for a day.

Good nutrition is only the starting point of ensuring maximum physical wellness. We also need to remain hydrated (i.e. drink plenty of water), get sufficient sleep, and exercise. The hydration part is fairly simple: keep a glass of water or water bottle with you at all times. If the water is there, you will naturally sip on it. It is very easy to drink 8 glasses of water a day when they are spread out over 16 hours. 4 ounces of water consumed over an hour goes unnoticed, whereas chugging 8 ounces 8 times a day can seem like a chore.

Sleep is perhaps a bit more challenging. Workaholics typically enter recovery with significant sleep deprivation. Alcoholics and other drug addicts may be more accustomed to passing out than falling asleep. Others may have relied on sleep medications to initiate sleep. Addicts seldom begin recovery with good sleep hygiene. Sleep hygiene refers to the behaviors and environments conducive to sleep. Good sleep hygiene includes avoiding caffeine, exercise, heavy meals and alcohol 4-6 hours before retiring to bed. In addition, it is helpful to establish a regular routine that leads up to the time you wish to sleep. For many, shutting off the television or computer, turning lights down, and reading relaxing literature is the ideal precursor to falling asleep. It is most beneficial to standardize your bedtimes. The more regular your sleep/wake cycle is, the more likely you are to enjoy a good night's rest. If you have had children or been around children, you will know what is most helpful in fostering sleep. Childcare providers know rest is critical for a child's wellness, both physical and emotional. Adults are no different. Apply the same tricks parents use to encourage their children to go to sleep to your own sleep rituals. There are many tools that can be used to improve sleep hygiene.

Once well nourished and rested, it is imperative that you engage in some type of physical exercise. Studies that identify the benefits of daily exercise have been replicated over and over. A daily regimen of 20 - 30 minutes of aerobic exercise can be the miracle cure for lethargy, elevated blood pressure, anxiety, depression, certain cardiac conditions, and weight problems. The benefit to emotional well being has also been well established (Sharma, 2006). If you are having trouble finding time for or maintaining consistency in your exercise routine, re-evaluate what you are trying to accomplish. If you are attempting an exercise program that you do not enjoy, there will be little motivation to carve out time for that activity. If you are planning exercise at the end of long business days, you are more likely to opt out than to opt in. Try to find an exercise that you enjoy (e.g. tennis, biking, yoga, dancing) and schedule it when you are likely to have both time and energy. The simplest way to create time for exercise is to wake up earlier each day. Develop a routine so that it will be integrated into your day-to-day life.

It is important to develop routines for every activity that supports your health and well being. If you have not already done so, establish daily, weekly, and monthly routines. Routines are wonderful. They allow us to simplify things. Without routines, even the most basic tasks would take on amazing complexity. When you have a routine for getting up each morning, you do not have to think about each step to start your day. For example: Imagine the complexity of getting dressed if you did not develop a routine. Each day new decisions would have to be made regarding when to dress, how to dress, which item of clothing to put on first, when to put your shoes on, which shoe to put on first, etc. Without weekly routines for self-sustaining activities, such as grocery shopping and laundry, it may be difficult to ensure you will have food to eat and clean clothes to wear. Routines for recovery meetings are also essential. While it is beneficial to explore new groups, having a home group and regular meetings promote continued engagement with recovery fellowships.

Routines support the immediate goals of maintaining the basic tasks of daily living. They apply to everyone. Consider the tasks you do on a daily, weekly, and monthly basis. Evaluate each to see if you already have schedules for those tasks. If not, set up routines to alleviate yourself from the continuous need for reminders and the frustrations when key tasks are forgotten. If you are not naturally organized or tend to have a lot going on, it will be helpful to write your planned routines on a calendar until they become automatic. After a period of time, you will naturally remember to pay the bills on the 20th or do laundry on Wednesday.

Unlike most immediate goals, which are common to many, short- and long-term goals must be highly individualized. These goals are based on your specific interests and passions, taking into consideration your unique qualities and characteristics. Yes, here it is ok, and in fact necessary, to claim your uniqueness. To maximize progress, it is necessary to develop plans to meet personal goals. Your goals are based entirely on what you have divined for self-fulfillment.

Short-term goals are goals you expect to achieve within the next 5 years. It is perhaps best to break those into "short-short" and "long-short" term goals. List your goals and prioritize their order. After you have prioritized the importance of these items, identify the time frame you will need to fulfill each. If you find any that can easily be completed, get working on them right away. If you find some that clearly require more than 5 years to complete, move them up to the long-term list. Making a list provides a structure to help complete your short-term goals. Next, develop a plan to achieve each goal.

For example: Your short-term goals include relocating to independent housing, finishing a degree, getting a new job and making more friends. These are all goals that can be completed within 5 years. If you wish to change your housing situation, you should first obtain a new job. While obtaining a new job, you are likely to meet new friends. Perhaps advanced training and/or education will help you get a new job and help you meet new friends. So the rank order for these goals might be: 1) Education or training, 2) New job, 3) New friends, and 4) A new and independent living situation. Now you can identify where to start and plan how you will complete these goals.

When you are satisfied with your short-term goals list, you can move forward to your long-term goals. Long-term goals can be limited to those you plan to finish in 5 to 10 years or goals you have for your lifetime. It is a matter of personal preference how many long-term goals you work on. You may have general long-term goals, such as remaining physically fit, which identifies the type of lifestyle you wish to live. It is possible to have many general long-term goals. Be careful, however, when listing specific long-term goals, such as completing college degrees or mastering trades. While you may wish to become a master carpenter, plumber, racecar driver and dentist; these skills require many years of education and/or training to become proficient. Setting multiple, specific long-term goals may be easier than selecting which ones are most important, but it is unrealistic. Long-term goals that can be achieved in 10 years should be sorted just as you did for the short-term goals – identify their priority and estimate the time needed to fulfill them. Once that is complete, you can develop a plan to reach each goal. Remember, seeing is believing. If you write the goals down, you are much more likely to move towards them.

Typical long-term goals include career achievement, owning a home and developing financial stability. Some long-term goals require concurrent attention. While you are advancing your career, you may be saving money to purchase a new home. Once the new home is purchased, you may continue saving towards other long-term goals. Long-term goals may interconnect. Earning more money may enable you to buy a home; however, if you are not judicious, you may neglect another long-term goal (e.g. saving for retirement). Many long-term goals interconnect and impact each other. Be careful in formulating your long-term goals. It is easy to set the bar so high that one goal cannot be met without compromising another. As you work to develop a plan, it will become apparent which goals can be reasonably achieved and which need to be modified. 10_S provides a structure that helps continuously monitor our progress. Goals that cannot be completed in 10 years are generally lifelong or lifestyle goals.

A word about lifelong goals: Envision! Just imagine what you wish to be 20 or 30 years from now. In the best of all possible worlds, what would you like to attract into your life? You will see it when you believe it! Believe it! Identify what you wish to do with your life in recovery and begin developing that life. If your goal is to leave a legacy through helping children, take each and every opportunity to be of service to them. That may mean being a nanny and inviting the friends of your children to visit whenever possible, helping children on a one-by-one basis. Or it may lead you to a teaching certificate, school administration, or training future teachers. Another person with the same goal may build schools in impoverished areas of the world. The list of possibilities is infinite.

Lifelong goals subtly inform our day-to-day life, allowing us to see opportunities, to move in the direction of our greatest good, to open doors that move us towards our goals. By identifying your goals, you will notice and take advantage of the opportunities which fulfill your dreams. You begin to live a purpose-driven life. Your growth continues as long as you stay willing to move forward and are careful to maintain a balance in recovery.

Step 8₅ Considerations

1. How is your health? Nutrition? Exercise schedule?

2. What is your first goal?

3. What is your plan to achieve your first goal?

4. Have you established daily, weekly and monthly routines?

5. Where would you like to be in 25 years? What do you expect to accomplish?

Step 9$_S$

Became willing to execute those plans whenever possible except when to do so might interfere with our recovery.

Our goals serve as a GPS for life once we identify them. GPS stands for global positioning system. If you fully developed your list of goals in 8$_S$, they will represent a global image, mapping out your future. The goals become a system, positioning us to take advantage of opportunities and follow paths to achieve our greatest good.

After you have divined your goals, shared them with another human being and set them down on paper, 9$_S$ is the next step. Plug them into your GPS, orient yourself to move in the direction of those goals. You will find that many opportunities present themselves if you are following your own compass. A chance meeting, a help wanted sign, a call for volunteers, a business with its door open, may all be opportunities to develop your future.

For example: If you have a goal to complete an apprenticeship in auto mechanics, you can be aware of any related people or places along your journey. Much like a GPS, you will be highlighting mechanics you meet, repair garages, technical institutes, and training centers. As you travel, your internal "screen" will depict each person or place along the way that might provide a related commodity or service. Much like the icons that appear when you MapQuest a physical destination, you will give special focus to anything related to a career destination: In this example, auto mechanics. As you meet people, you will bypass the teachers, poets, and servers, and hone in on others in your chosen career. If you see a "red dot" (aka another mechanic) you will stop and talk, exploring your opportunities.

If one of your short term goals is to repair your home, then position yourself to move in that direction. A few spare moments become an opportunity to research trades people needed to assist in the repairs. When casual conversation reveals a neighbor's cousin just started his own construction business, you ask for the contact information instead of changing the topic. A random comment overheard in Home Depot will alert you to a closeout on paint. The often overlooked sign listing "do-it-yourself" classes now becomes a source of important information. Before you know it, you are installing a new floor. Once your GPS is set on the next destination, items related to that goal will be more relevant and draw you to them.

Have you always wanted to be a nurse but dropped out of the 11th grade? Put it on your list, and keep your eyes and ears open. In 12-step fellowships, you may meet other people who also failed to complete high school. Not everyone recognizes the power they have to manage their lives in sobriety. Some do not set goals to "re-cover" past opportunities; they continue to accept limitations imposed on them during active addiction. In recovery, things can be different! There are adult education programs to help prepare for the GED. In most states, a high school diploma (or its equivalent) allows you to enter community college. Some community colleges have nursing programs. They also can provide a gradual transition into professional study at universities. Too old, you say? If you are under 80 years old, I believe you are *too young* to passively accept unfulfilled dreams. One of my favorite books is *The Little Engine that Could* (Piper, 1976). If you have not read it, you should. The little engine saved the circus not by brawn or cunning, but by believing he could and trying. So just say to yourself, "I think I can. I think I can. I think I can." You will be amazed. One day, you will find yourself saying, "I thought I could. I thought I could," when you reach your goals. The key to fulfilling your dreams is having a plan and believing you can do it. Once those two elements are in place, you can position yourself to succeed.

People change in two ways, proactively and reactively. The proactive individual goes out and finds what he or she needs. The reactive person prefers to wait until he or she encounters something, and then reacts to it. The most successful change agents move proactively forward, trying to minimize surprises and avoid situations that call for reacting. Thinking proactively allows you to anticipate what might happen and plan for it. This is not to suggest that we can know everything about what might happen in the future. It is to recommend that we anticipate the possibilities and make tentative plans for how to manage them. Even when we cannot predict what is going to happen, proactive thinkers respond with action that may improve situations or make the best out of an unplanned event. For example: Sarena discovered after months of working to purchase a house that the deal would not go through. After a few hours of upset, she began moving forward, considering other options. Within a week, she had found a home much better suited for her family. In another instance, John had been volunteering at a retirement home for several months, hoping to get hired. He was crestfallen when someone else was chosen. That very day, the daughter of one of the residents saw John fixing a cabinet and asked where he worked. He told her that he was volunteering to keep himself busy while looking for work. The next day, the woman contacted John with a job offer. Sarena and John both handled disappointment in proactive ways. They moved forward making the best of each situation.

Proactive thinkers make lemonade out of lemons. They are flexible, looking for alternatives and finding ways around obstacles. Reactive thinkers, on the other hand, tend to be rigid and inflexible. They experience life as a series of surprises. The reactive thinker is frequently derailed from their schedule or activity by something that was unanticipated. Without a goal or direction, it is easy to be blown off course. For the spontaneous, carefree type this is not a big deal. They seem to enjoy the mystery of life. But those who wish to reach their goals must stay focused on creating the change they wish to see. Proactive thinkers want to move forward, grabbing experience and opportunity. They always see how a situation or event can be used in a positive way. A proactive thinker with a goal and a plan is very likely to succeed. If you are willing to be proactive, you will be following **g**ood **o**rderly **d**irection.

The only caveat to this process is to ensure that you protect your recovery along the way. The way we protect our recovery is the same way we established it in the first place. Follow the original 12 Steps:

1. Recognize that your life can become unmanageable and you are powerless over your addictive illness.

2. Use whatever power you recognize outside yourself to assure you continue to approach the world in a sane manner.

3. Allow God and others to provide care and direction.

4. Stay on the lookout for past behavior patterns that might signal a possible relapse.

5. Share with others your imperfections.

6. Identify those character defects which might return to disrupt your progress.

7. Ask others to let you know if your shortcomings start to show.

8. If you have feelings of guilt for things you have done, be willing to make amends.

9. Make those amends so you can move on with your life.

10. Continue to take spot-check inventories to ensure you stay on track, make corrections as needed.

11. Stay focused on what supports your recovery and do the next right thing.

12. Represent! Practice the principles of recovery in all your affairs. Let others know that it can be done.

While you are continuing to work these 12 Steps, *keep going to meetings!* Old timers say they go to meetings to find out what happens to people who do not go to meetings. Meetings remind us of what it was like. Seeing a newcomer walk through the door will remind you of how bad it was and how bad it could be again.

Anyone who has emerged from addictive illness knows the feelings of being in the abyss. Unfortunately, it can be difficult to recognize the precursors to relapse before it is too late. After a few years of sobriety, we may be lulled into a false sense of security, feeling we are no longer at risk. Dis-ease combined with life struggles, however, may set us up for relapse. If drugs, food, alcohol, sex, work, gambling, etc. worked once to escape uncomfortable feelings, they will work again. In relapse, we are no longer at ease with ourselves or others. Problems begin to overwhelm us and stress mounts. Emotionally, we find ourselves out of sorts, depressed, irritable, anxious, and reactive, struggling to cope. We question the need and/or ability to stay in recovery. As these negative feelings mount, we avoid the happy, joyous and free people found in the 12-Step rooms. We begin to isolate. In isolation, we often let go of our routines, forget our goals and plans, eat inappropriately, exercise less and suffer ill health. Our resources dwindle physically, mentally, emotionally and spiritually. Going to meetings keeps us connected to healthy, sober people and recovery tools. Meetings remind us that we will always be at risk but, in recovery, we do have the capacity to live life on life's terms. Attending meetings helps protect against relapse.

Dr. Terrance Gorski is world-renowned for his research and writing on the issue of relapse in addictive disorders. His many books, videos, trainings and lectures provide invaluable insight into relapse. Please check out the resources on his website, www.relapse. org. Another valuable resource is the AWARE (Advanced Warning of Relapse) questionnaire that was developed through research funded by the National Institute on Alcohol Abuse and Alcoholism (NIAAA, contract ADM 281-91-0006) (Miller, 2000). The AWARE is a 28 item test that surveys symptoms and provides scoring to predict the probability of relapse. This and other tools like it are sometimes useful as a checklist to assure you are not falling back into addictive behavior patterns.

One of the best antidotes for relapse is a wonder-full life in recovery. That is the purpose of *The Sequel*. By employing the Sequel Steps, your life expands beyond imagination. In establishing goals and growing, you will find you have too much to lose to risk relapse. When you are actively engaged in creating the things you want in your life, you will stay focused on recovery. You need to maintain a balance. As you succeed in growing and changing, you could digress and regress. To avoid backsliding and to maximize your potential, you will need to work the 10_sth step.

Step 9_s Considerations

1. Do you have a "can do" attitude?

2. In what situations do you most often react?

3. How can you become more proactive?

4. What is most likely to threaten your sobriety?

5. What tools can you regularly employ to protect your recovery and avoid relapse?

Step 10$_S$

Continued to monitor our progress, making adjustments as needed to assure maximum benefit for ourselves and others.

The 7th habit of Stephen R. Covey's *Seven Habits of Highly Effective People* (Covey, 1989) focuses on keeping a balance between producing and renewing one's capacity to produce. Covey includes physical, emotional and spiritual renewal in his 7th habit; those elements are addressed in Steps 3$_S$, 7$_S$, and 8$_S$. Step 10$_S$ focuses on maintaining a balance. In the original 10th step, we looked at what we did wrong and promptly admitted it. Here we look at what we are doing right and make certain we are staying on course.

Having completed 8$_S$, we can easily construct an inventory list of what we expect to manifest in our future. Yes, it really is simple. KISMIF! Look at your immediate goals, things like maintaining health and wellness. Add those items to a daily inventory. These lay the foundation for future growth and development.

For example:

Slept a minimum of 7-8 hours   ____

Exercised today   ____

Ate nutritionally and/or took vitamins   ____

Next look at your short term goals:

For example:

Applied to school   ____

Added to savings to buy a home   ____

Applied for a new job/promotion   ____

Long term goals may or may not have elements that should be addressed on a daily basis. Add those that do to your inventory.

For example:

Continued to be honest in all my affairs   ____

Remained available to my family   ____

Contributed to my retirement fund   ____

Lifelong goals generally reflect a social duty to provide for future generations. This obligation generates goals focused on improving one's personal contribution to the world. Social psychologists have long recognized the importance a sense of accomplishment is to life satisfaction. Professional development, self-fulfillment and personal integrity are a few of the items that might be found on a checklist of lifelong goals. Other ideas can be found in any daily meditation book and the "Just for Today" suggestions found within Narcotics Anonymous (NA), Alcoholics Anonymous (AA) and Al-Anon.

The NA reading (Narcotics Anonymous, 1986) focuses most directly on activities to sustain recovery. Its concepts are summarized in the following list:

Focused on recovery   ____

Enjoyed life without using addictively   ____

Contacted friends who support recovery   ____

Followed my recovery program   ____

Acted in faith not fear   ____

A "Just for Today" card can often be found in AA and Al-Anon meetings. It is adapted from a poem written by Sybil F. Partridge in 1916 and printed in *How To Stop Worrying, And Start Living* (Carnegie, 1951). It lists 9 ways to improve our attitude and outlook on life (written in italics below). I invite you to consider these items in part of your 10_s^{th} step inventory as well.

- *Just for today I will try to live through this day only, and not tackle all my problems at once. I can do something for twelve hours that would appall me if I felt that I had to keep it up for a lifetime.*

This is a difficult one for many of us. Beset by guilt and vestiges of our past, it is often hard not to ruminate on "back when", but it is most necessary to stay focused on the present. We have changed. We are not the same people we were before recovery. If we do the next right thing, one step at a time, we can accomplish a great deal. If we worry about the future and all its unknowns, we often get distracted from the present. As you review your day, consider the question, "Did I keep my head where my feet were?"

- *Just for today I will be happy. This assumes to be true what Abraham Lincoln said, that most folks are as happy as they make up their minds to be.*

This might be a novel concept for someone new to recovery, who does not understand the principle of self-determination. Anyone who has participated in 12 Step meetings for a few months realizes the power we have to determine our approach to life. Even if we have suffered tragic losses, we can choose to focus on what we have left. Using this concept for our 10_S^{th} Step helps us see the positive in every day. Even when we rumble and grumble through the day, our inventory can be reframed to reflect those elements that were good. When we look at the good, we feel good as well.

- *Just for today I will adjust myself to what is, and not try to adjust everything to my own desires. I will take my luck as it comes, and fit myself to it.*

Accepting life on life's terms can sometimes be a challenge. Did we adjust ourselves to events of the day? Or whine and complain, angry that things did not go our way? Remember, God sometimes writes straight using crooked lines. Even when things have not gone the way we would like, they may have set the stage for something even greater. As we approach each day, we evaluate what opportunities are present. They may not be the ones we originally anticipated, but they may offer new opportunities. If we keep our goals in mind, we can find ways that the unexpected can enhance our progress. When we review the day, we will see the benefit of adjusting to opportunities that are presented to us.

- *Just for today I will try to strengthen my mind. I will study. I will learn something useful. I will not be a mental loafer. I will read something that requires effort, thought and concentration.*

Many find the focused concentration of reading very difficult in early recovery. Hopefully by the time we are working 10_S, our cognitive capacity has improved and we can begin expanding our minds. As we move towards satisfying the goals listed in 8_S, we may need to do some research, read manuals or study textbooks. It is always of benefit to challenge our minds. Doing so improves the health of our brain. It has been well established and substantiated that an active mind stays functional much longer than an inactive mind. Each day we need to challenge ourselves. This is not a place to set standards of perfection. Doing anything new, making a new recipe, going to an art show and creative writing, all counts. The brain needs the stimulation of a novel situation in order to continue developing.

- *Just for today I will exercise my soul in three ways: I will do somebody a good turn, and not get found out; if anybody knows of it, it will not count. I will do at least two things I don't want to do just for exercise. I will not show anyone that my feelings are hurt; they may be hurt, but today I will not show it.*

This one is a tall order for anyone, in or out of recovery. Initially, it will seem difficult to do something for someone without getting found out. Once we take on this challenge, however, we find it is relatively easy. The longer we work at doing this, the more natural it becomes. Things we might do: A housemate leaves a dish in the sink – we put it in the dishwasher. A co-worker forgets an important task – we notice and complete the job. We can drop some money in a donation box, move a grocery cart back to the corral or pick up a piece of litter. Any task we take on that makes life easier or safer for another human being improves the world, regardless of whether we receive recognition or not. Practice random acts of kindness.

When we take on the challenge of doing two things we do not want to do, typically the tasks we choose are things that need to be done. The chores we do not want to do may not be critical for survival, but when they are done, they improve our living conditions. Certainly most housekeeping tasks could be considered for this list, but so might writing thank-you notes or exercising. The Sequel is about living life optimally in recovery. This sometimes entails doing things that we do not particularly want to do in order to improve our lives.

The last suggestion of this section may seem confusing, as it suggests we should not share our feelings. This reflects the probability that if our feelings are hurt, it is usually a result of someone else's behavior. Hurt feelings are often more about our unmet expectations than about another's bad behavior. If we refrain from expressing hurt feelings, it prevents us from placing blame on others. We take responsibility for our feelings. We live and let live.

- *Just for today I will be agreeable. I will look as well as I can, dress becomingly, keep my voice low, be courteous, criticize not one bit. I won't find fault with anything, nor try to improve or regulate anybody but myself.*

Be agreeable! This means having a pleasant demeanor and rolling with the flow. We focus on the only part of life we can truly change – ourselves! It **is** all about us and how we choose to face the world. We do not need to waste time with criticism or try to regulate or improve anyone else. Working on ourselves gives us plenty to do.

In addictive illness, we are often so wrapped up in our own agenda that we fail to take care of our appearance. When under the influence, it did not seem to matter what we looked like. We were so anxious to place a bet, over exercise, get to the grocery or liquor store that we did not care. In recovery, we should set aside time for grooming and presenting a good image to the world. The reception we receive from others will reflect how we look. Life seems to go slightly better if we are dressed becomingly. When we take time to look our best, the reflection of the guy or gal in the glass will be affirming.

- *Just for today I will have a program. I may not follow it exactly, but I will have it. I will save myself from two pests: hurry and indecision.*

This entire book discusses how important it is to have a program – a set of instructions to help guide our lives. In chapter 8, we spoke about the importance of goal setting and having a direction. In chapter 9, we discussed following our plans unless to do so would endanger our recovery. It was recommended that we maintain a balance and follow **g**ood **o**rderly **d**irection. By following the path that leads to our greatest good and having a game plan, we can avoid indecision. If we have a clear sense of where we are going and a certainty that we can get there, we do not need to hurry.

- *Just for today I will have a quiet half hour all by myself and relax. During this half hour, sometime, I will try to get a better perspective on my life.*

Taking time for oneself is imperative. Some will complain that a half hour is too long to commit to relaxing and being quiet. I believe it is a bare minimum. People who know me might laugh and think it impossible that I apportion such time to myself, but that is because it is woven into my daily schedule. The secret is to weave relaxation and self-reflection time into our daily lives. This may be easier to do when we live alone; it may require some explanation or negotiation if we live with others. Family and friends will understand if we gently explain that we are taking some quiet time and wish not to be disturbed. The simplest way to find this time is to get up early, before everyone else awakens. It is a great way to start the day.

- *Just for today I will be unafraid. Especially, I will not be afraid to enjoy what is beautiful and to believe that as I give to the world, so the world will give to me.*

Addiction usually exposes us to many negative consequences, creating difficult relationships and often leading to a pessimistic view of the world. In recovery, we generally find hope and more optimistic viewpoints, but there may be some lingering fear. What would happen if we stopped being afraid? Most of us live in areas where we are not in imminent danger of losing our lives or being hurt. So why are we afraid? Books have been written about fear-based cultures. The United States media has been particularly focused on the potential dangers in our lives since September 11, 2001. But what if we refused to listen and simply "pretended" all was well and we were ok? Suddenly life would look much better.

Going a step further, what if we actually believed that the Golden Rule represented a universal principle, that whatever we sowed we would reap 10 fold? Throughout history there is documentation of the power of positive thinking. Act as a change agent. Just be nice. In my local community, one caring citizen has mounted a "just be nice" campaign. The billboards, bumper stickers, bus ads and other marketing items are everywhere, reminding people to just be nice. What a great concept! Just be nice and we will improve the lives of those around us and, in turn, our own.

It takes a great deal of stamina and determination to complete the first 10 Steps of the Sequel, but the results are well worth the effort. Step 11_S helps us stay on track.

Step 10$_S$ Considerations

1. Have you prepared your 10$_S$ lists? Are you using them?

2. Do you stay focused on the present?

3. Did you challenge your mind today?

4. Have you been flexible and able to adjust your activities and time schedules?

5. Do you try to be the best person you can be on a daily basis?

Step 11$_S$

Sought through prayer and meditation to improve our conscious contact with God, as we understand God, praying only for the knowledge of God's will for us and the power to carry that out.

Many people reserve prayer for times when they have a need. The word, itself, seems to connote asking for or wanting something. What is beautiful about the 11th Step is that it recommends prayer to gain both knowledge and strength. It specifically cautions us to pray only for those things. To pray for specifics can be limiting or counterproductive. For example: An incarcerated man once prayed for patience. When it was time for the parole board to review his case, they found outstanding warrants and sentenced him to another five years. A young mother prayed for the quick birth of her firstborn child and shortly thereafter was scheduled for an emergency C-section. This is not to suggest that there is a divine being micromanaging our lives and acting on each individual prayer. It is to point out that sometimes we cannot foresee what is in our own best interest. If we pray for knowledge, it opens us up to receiving new ideas. If we pray for the strength to handle certain situations, and believe prayers are answered, we presume we will have the strength we need. This becomes a self-fulfilling prophecy – by believing we have the power, we find it. A slogan frequently heard in 12-Step fellowships is that God doesn't give us more than we can handle. Many recovering people believe this to be fact. As a result, they approach difficulties with a willingness to persevere and a resolve to find solutions.

Making the statement, "God doesn't give us more than we can handle" is a prayer of affirmation. It affirms that life will not overwhelm us. It is an affirmation that we have the ability to manage whatever struggles we face. What harm can be done by affirming we have capability? Prayers of affirmation reassure us that the God of our understanding is working within us and in our lives. Achieving abstinence and completing the 12 Steps was empowering. We have sufficient experience to affirm that God is doing for us what we could not do for ourselves. Affirmative prayer reminds us that we are on a spiritual path, awakening our energies to achieve our greatest good.

If you are not accustomed to using prayers of affirmation, please take some time and consider what you might affirm in your recovery. Perhaps you will affirm that God provides the knowledge of His will for you and the power to carry that out. Maybe you will affirm that divine intelligence guides your every thought, word, and action. Some might affirm the ability to reach lifelong goals. For example: "I am guided and strengthened to complete my education/retire by age 65/win an Oscar." Whatever you desire to bring into your life, you may affirm its presence now or in the future. If you have the attitude that there is more, that you can be more and have more, then you will get more. This is not meant to refer to more "stuff", but rather to personal growth. Material things may come along as well, but it will be secondary to personal happiness. For years I have heard addicts referred to as people who can never get enough, as if it were a derogatory trait. How sad to think of a zest for living, for growing and gathering more experiences, might be considered harmful. Affirmation reflects optimism and the belief that you can and will succeed. Be a way-shower. Seldom do we stop moving forward if we believe we can. It is all in the attitude. Affirm that you can, and will, be more than you are today.

The concept behind the 11th step is to connect with a power greater than your ordinary self in order to gain knowledge and strength. Whether you ascribe the knowledge to divine communication, forces of nature, or other human beings, by petitioning for assistance, we consider information from outside ourselves. Conversely, meditative practices are all designed to turn the focus inward, to take quiet time to increase our awareness of the power within ourselves. We expand our autonomy through meditation and prayer. By seeking knowledge and power, we increase our freedom and expand our opportunities for growth.

The 11th step must be taken individually. Each person is challenged to identify methods of prayer and meditation that best suit their needs. Those with religious affiliation may find tools through their faith traditions. Many religious institutions have standardized prayers as part of their rituals. The AA Big Book recommends a scripted prayer for the 11th Step. It is the Prayer of St. Francis (Alcoholics Anonymous World Services, Inc., 2001, p. 99). For those who are uncertain about how to pray or what to pray for, the Prayer of St. Francis is a good way to begin. It is a simple prayer that petitions to be guided to love, sow peace, heal hurts, have faith and be joyful. Who could dispute the value of asking for those opportunities?

The 11th Step centers our growth. Meditation helps us maintain balance. It reminds us to stop and pay attention to what is going on in our lives. How often have we forged ahead maniacally, racing into a brick wall (figuratively or literally)? Addictive behavior is obsessive-compulsive. In our disease we were accustomed to obsessing about getting high/thin/rich/smarter/etc. In our recovery, most of us still tend to be somewhat obsessive and compulsive. Working the Sequel Steps, being empowered to reach for new goals and expand horizons, we may be tempted to obsess over those goals. When we obsess, we often feel compelled to take action. It is not uncommon for people with a passion to forget about other areas of their lives while obsessively and compulsively pursuing their goals. If we take time to practice step 11_s, it will naturally slow us down (at least temporarily) and allow us time to re-assess.

When we meditate we listen. During meditative periods, we can release our preconceived notions and allow our thoughts to flow freely. Without the imposition of logic and reason, the mind is free to reconfigure knowledge into new ideas. For those in transition, meditation may point towards a new goal or allow insight, enabling you to envision life transformations. As the book title says, "You'll See It When You Believe It" (Dyer, 1989). Theists attribute the thoughts and feelings that arise during meditation to divine inspiration. Others view meditation as quiet time used to sort through one's own ideas and emotions. No matter your spiritual preferences, the mindfulness of meditation is a centering experience. Meditation involves reflection and contemplation.

There are many types of meditation. Transcendental Meditation (TM) is the most widely studied form and, therefore, a good place to start. TM creates a state of restful alertness that is believed to allow access to a transcendent consciousness of the innermost self. Practiced 20 minutes per day with eyes closed, the meditating individual clears the mind by thinking of the sound of a mantra. The goal is to experience a silent and peaceful level of consciousness. Other restful forms of meditation rely on focusing attention on sounds, sights, or breath. In meditation, we focus on one stimulus and do not attend to other elements in our surroundings. A wide variety of recordings are available that provide instrumental or natural sounds to facilitate meditation. A landscape, picture, or candle flame may also be used to cone down our attention into a meditative trance. The simplest tool is to focus on our breath as it rocks back and forth, in and out. The goal of meditation is to stop attending to the external environment in order to attend to the internal environment.

For some, the still, quiet forms of meditation are difficult, creating anxiety instead of relaxation. If you are one of those types, you might do best with an action-based meditative practice. One popular form is Tai Chi. Developed as a form of self-defense, in modern times Tai Chi is more commonly practiced as moving meditation. The emphasis on repetitive motions, learned in a specific sequence and form, draws your focus inward. There are also many forms of walking meditations. Labyrinths are often used to symbolize the path into the center of your Self as well as your path back into the world. If there is a meditative labyrinth in your area, you may try using it as a guide for walking meditation. As with all meditative practices, moving meditations encourage an increased internal awareness to improve perception and knowledge.

It is helpful after a period of meditation to take out a pad and do some journaling. Journaling can serve to record thoughts and awarenesses that came to mind during meditation. As we journal across the line and down the page, we often achieve greater clarity and perception. The most productive way to journal is to write in a stream of consciousness. Stream of consciousness means you simply write what comes to mind. It allows you to sidestep the rational, organized and sometimes obsessive mind and explore other random, subconscious ideas that may highlight important issues. To write in such an unstructured fashion may take practice, but it is worth the effort. After you have written for a period of time, review what was written. Journaling can be akin to meditation as new ideas pop out on paper and increase your awareness.

Step 11 is designed to provide new insight and direction. The *Twelve Steps and Twelve Traditions* (Alcoholics Anonymous World Services, Inc., 2001, p. 105) identifies a "sense of belonging" which comes from working this step. I believe that sense of belonging emanates from a connectedness we achieve within ourselves, through meditation and journaling, and beyond ourselves through prayer. It is as if the 11th Step fills in the space between the individual and the greater universe.

There is no need to get caught up with questions about whether there is or is not a God. The only thing you need to know about God is that you ain't it. It is a power greater than yourself; that is all you need to know. It makes no difference whether it be physics or a being with flowing hair and a staff sitting on a throne. Step 11 simply asks that you stop, consider new information, and carry on. *Do not complicate this simple program!*

Step 11$_S$ Considerations

1. What is your usual manner of praying?

2. Develop a list of affirmative prayers to support your Sequel work.

3. What is your preferred manner of meditation?

4. When do you meditate?

5. If you do not have an established meditative practice, begin one now.

Step 12$_S$

Having had a spiritual experience as the result of these steps we carried this message to others so they might continue to grow and improve their lives.

Spread the word! The 12th Step suggests we carry the message to others who are suffering. Meetings become motivational in new ways. 12$_S$ provides an opportunity to carry a message to others as they continue on a path of discovery in recovery. Having regained a sense of purpose, discovering a destiny and developing new skills revitalizes our spirit. We will have new visions for the future. We will take our message of hope and change into the recovery rooms, encouraging others to continue growing. It is important to share our experience, strength and hope. Many people will recognize the amazing capacity they have to change their lives once they take back their power in sobriety.

Tell your story. Let others know what it was like when you began your recovery and how you have changed through working the 12 Steps and the Sequel Steps. Share the benefits of sobriety. If Bill Wilson and Bob Smith had not been willing to grow and change,

Alcoholics Anonymous and all other 12 Step programs would not exist. They shared their experience with the world so others could benefit. 12_s asks you to do the same.

The Big Book, *Alcoholics Anonymous,* (Alcoholics Anonymous World Services, Inc., 2001) identifies rewards that materialize as a result of working the steps. The promises, listed after Step 9, say we will experience "a new freedom and a new happiness." The freedom is obvious. It is the result of our release from the bondage of addiction. The happiness comes in waves and only builds as you complete the steps. By completing the Sequel, you extend that happiness to its maximum level. We will no longer look back with shame and regret at our past life; we will be grateful to have escaped the obsessive compulsivity of addictive behavior. We will have gratitude. We will realize that our lives would have turned out very differently if we had not found the 12 Steps. In recovery we experience serenity. The third step teaches us to let go of the outcome so that we may remain peaceful as our lives evolve. We can focus on ourselves and let go of the desire to control others, accepting their right to follow their own path. We can live comfortably and without conflict. As the chaos in our heads quiets down, the chaos around us will cease. We are right with the world and in harmony with our true selves. We are at ease in our own skin. We are okay.

If we practice the 12th Step in its original and Sequel form, we will see how our experience can benefit others. By sharing our initial recovery from addiction, we assure others that they too can achieve abstinence. No longer compulsively seeking pleasure, we model our life on personal growth and well-being. The goal of the Sequel is to flourish and enjoy life. We become role models for anyone who doubts the human capacity to change. We attract others to this new way of approaching life. We challenge them to identify and manifest their skills, talents and abilities.

Old timers may be concerned that the Sequel promotes self-serving independence to the neglect of the greater good. That is simply not true. The greater good is not served by immobility and stagnation. Failure to grow diminishes motivation and well-being. Humans have an inherent tendency to learn, explore and develop their potential (Ryan, 2000). Sobriety provides us an opportunity to resume our cognitive and social development. To identify and master our talents, to achieve new goals, is a mandate. We honor and respect our recovering fellowships by using the gifts of sobriety to fulfill our potential. We rejoice in our accomplishments. We have a responsibility to carry this message to others. "Our whole attitude and outlook upon life will change" (Alcoholics Anonymous World Services, Inc., 2001, p. 84).

Those who have worked the Sequel Steps know how wonder-full life can be. It is important to let others know. "The majority of 'normal' people also need examples and advice to reach a richer and more fulfilling existence" (Seligman, 2000). The Sequel 12 Steps guide us to getting well and fully enjoying life. Developing competence, autonomy and relatedness are the key components of personal growth and well-being (Ryan, 2000). Challenge others to employ the power they have to manage their own lives. Let them know what it was like before and what it is like now, flourishing in recovery. Encourage others to find their bliss. Everyone will benefit when they work the Sequel Steps and experience happiness and success beyond their wildest dreams. Enjoy the journey as you continue along the road of happy destiny.

Step 12$_\text{S}$ Considerations

1. Do you share your achievements as a result of your recovery?

2. Do you encourage others to continue improving their lives?

3. What improvements have you made since beginning these steps?

4. What goals remain?

5. Write affirmations to support your continued growth.

Afterword

I implore you to keep things simple and make them fun in your recovery. If it gets too complicated, you could lose focus and enthusiasm. Getting clean and sober was difficult, but growing in recovery can be fun. We did not get sober to be miserable!

Working the original steps releases us from the bondage of addiction. Bill Wilson recognized that there needed to be more. He addressed that fact in a 1958 submission to the Grapevine entitled, "The Next Frontier: Emotional Sobriety." He pondered how our unconscious could be altered to rid itself of the toxicity from the past, to allow us to obtain what "we actually believe, know and want." That is why we need to work both sets of steps. The first set focuses on recovery, eliminating the toxicity of our addictions. The Sequel Steps keep us moving in a positive direction toward what we believe, know and want.

This is a simple program. Dr. Bob's continuing refrain was to keep it simple. Take the concepts and tailor them to you. Use your own words. No need to memorize or quote the book; simply use the tools and practice the principles. We are powerful beyond our imagination. We are brilliant, beautiful, talented, and fabulous. Sobriety allows us to enjoy life to its fullest.

Just make sure you…

Keep it simple, make it fun!

Acknowledgements

This book could not have been written without the accumulated knowledge and support of thousands of recovering individuals who passed on their legacies of experience, strength, and hope. Hundreds of those folks have personally touched my life, too many to identify. Some names have been forgotten or, perhaps, never known. Thank you to all who have gone before me.

A very special appreciation goes to my daughter, Beth, who continued to believe in me and this project. Our family may be small but it is mighty!

With gratitude for the many recovering friends and acquaintances who encouraged me to continue writing. Special thanks to Beth, Cindy, Elizabeth, Esther, Gary, Jack, Kelley, and Lin who read the draft and helped edit the final copy. No doubt we missed something, but then again we are not perfect, only striving for perfection.

APPENDIX A

MY STORY

The 12 step Sequel solidifies some of the components of my own recovery which led me to succeed in most of my affairs. I include my story as an appendix rather than infuse it throughout the book. This book is not about me, but rather about a process I applied and have taught for many years. My recovery program teaches me to share my experience, strength and hope, so I include the following as a testimony to the process. Hopefully it will give you some insight as to how the Sequel Steps work.

I was born 5 weeks premature. At the time they believed preemies would remain small and possibly limited intellectually for the rest of their lives. I grew to be 5'11 ½ inches tall and have completed three college degrees. I have reason to discount negative predictions!

Both my parents were alcoholic and took lots of prescription pills. By most people's standards I was neglected, but I didn't know any better so it didn't bother me. I roamed my hometown making friends with the owner of the candy store, stopping by to visit friends' parents, and walking to church to be nurtured by the secretary and a nascent faith. In retrospect, I realize I was collecting bits of parenting from anyone available. School was my favorite place because I could do well and receive acknowledgement. Academic achievement was the only indication I had that I might have any value. At age 12, I experienced my first bout with hopelessness. I don't recall what sparked my sense that life was not worth living, but I do remember considering suicide. I have a potentially fatal drug allergy to a medicine that was readily available at the time. The thought of taking it consumed me. Eventually, I asked my mother to remove it from my reach and she did. There were no questions asked and no recognition that I was sad.

By age 12, I started smoking cigarettes that I would steal from my parents. They never noticed. Later, when I would steal money from my mother's wallet, it went unnoticed as well. In fact, I went unnoticed most of my life. In 6th grade, all of my friends left our school for a special gifted program. I was invited but my father would not let me go. Left back with kids I barely knew, I found a crowd that smoked, kissed boys, drank and stole things from stores. In order to fit in, I did the same things they did. I didn't like the taste of alcohol, but I was particularly fond of a cough syrup with codeine. I remember feigning a cough as I signed for the syrup at the local pharmacy. I had found my first drug to escape reality.

Middle school was uneventful with the possible exception of my first love. It raised a ruckus in my hometown. He was from Sri Lanka and had very dark skin. I delighted in the rebellion, the attention and him. We stayed together for several years, but ultimately he left because of my addiction.

In high school, I began drinking, smoked anything that would get me high, and continued using the cough syrup. I brought alcohol to school for classroom parties and football games. I drank in the living room with my parents on a regular basis. They didn't notice since they were usually drunk themselves. Fortunately, I continued to get good grades. It was the only thing that kept me believing I was ok.

My parents thought I should go to the local community college and become a kindergarten teacher. Instead, I conspired with the high school guidance counselor and applied to the New College program at Hofstra University. I was accepted. To win my parents support, I agreed to graduate in 3 years instead of 4. I left Marblehead and Puritan Road to a much broader social network where the drinking age was 18 and marijuana was plentiful. With the independence of being away from home, I quickly established myself in a "partying crowd." I partied with the best of them. One night we decided to have a "smoke-off" to determine who had the highest tolerance. I didn't fold. Twelve hours after we started, Gary and I conceded it was a tie. I know now that my tolerance was both a blessing and a curse. A curse because it foretold a debilitating progression of my addiction, but a blessing because I still functioned reasonably well for several more years.

I did well enough in my undergraduate program to be invited to student teach the third year. The next year, I entered graduate school and stayed on as a teaching intern at the University. The door opened and I walked through it. I'd never had plans to teach, didn't feel comfortable in front of a classroom, and was having trouble getting to morning classes after getting drunk the night before, but there was an opportunity so I took it.

After completing my Master's degree, I was hired as an Instructor of Psychology. It was the mid-70's, women were still a minority in academia. There was talk of glass ceilings but I didn't pay much attention. No one told me I shouldn't or couldn't do what I was doing, so I just did it. Along the way, I decided to add an "Mrs." to the BA and Ms. Ed. I married the first man that asked. I was young, often under the influence, and not at all prepared to be married. Our differences were too extreme; after a couple years, we divorced. Shortly thereafter, I resigned my teaching position. I couldn't seem to manage my work responsibilities - drugs and alcohol were overtaking career and intellect.

Rather than attribute my difficulties to addiction, I decided the problem was a lack of practical experience. I moved to Maryland where I found a job and an apartment at a residential treatment program for adolescents. Why not? I might not have felt able to teach college, but surely I could guide emotionally disturbed youth. I worked the early morning shift, got high, slept, worked the evening shift, got drunk, slept, got up and did it all over again. The schedule was 4 days on and 3 days off. My supervisor made sure we had the same days off and we often drank from midnight 'til dawn together. I took one day at a time, recognizing that life's a bitch and then you die. I changed jobs a few times, each time my supervisor moved with me. Eventually, we married. It seemed to make sense. We were constant companions. We had no physical intimacy but I rationalized that it assured the relationship was based on friendship rather than prurient interests. (This decision was later to be one of the hallmarks of the insanity of my addiction)

After just a couple years of poly-substance dependence, I became unemployed and unemployable. Dejected, in a loveless marriage, terrified to talk to anyone, unable to stay clean and sober for more than a day, I prepared my suicide altar. I remember the peace I felt knowing that my struggles would end with my life; it seemed like a logical solution. But, I had always been one to explore all options. It occurred to me that if I stopped drinking, maybe things would get better. I had taught an undergraduate addiction course and recalled reading stories about how self-help groups had changed people's lives. I wanted the option to test both alternatives: death and sobriety. That meant trying a support group before suicide. If that didn't work, if my life didn't get better, I still had the option to escape my misery. I called a friend in recovery and started attending meetings. The recovering community welcomed me with open arms, saying they would love me until I loved myself. Ha! I thought. They have no idea. I don't even know myself. Little did I realize, they did have an idea. Everyone had been where I had been, beaten to a pulp physically and emotionally, before they walked into a 12-step room.

Getting clean and sober was not easy for me, there was no pink cloud. I was unemployed and too afraid to file for unemployment. The creditors were calling, ready to repossess my car with only 3 payments remaining. We were about to get evicted. Fortunately, I had achieved a small amount of power to manage my life and was learning to do the next right thing. I spoke to our landlord, terminated the lease, and found a room to rent. Once sober, it was obvious the marriage had been a foolish decision made in an addicted stupor. I filed for divorce and unemployment. Initially, my sponsor and groups of drunks in meetings were my higher power. Then one day, I humbly asked God to help guide me in finding a job. When I arrived home, there was a telephone message from Sister MaryAnn. She had a job offer. To attribute this coincidence to random chance seemed unlikely. Thus, I began believing in God.

The job was a Unit Supervisor for emotionally disturbed adolescents. I felt like a teenager myself, but I needed work. Having prayed and asked for guidance, I reasoned that if I was divinely directed I would be divinely empowered. I *sought through prayer and meditation to improve my conscious contact with God, as I understood God, praying only for the knowledge of God's will for me and the power to carry that out.* I went to work praying and left praying. I may not have been sure there was a God, but believing there was helped, so that's what I did. I spent a little over 2 years at that job, establishing my recovery and being emotionally supported by co-workers and recovering friends. Despite stellar employment reviews, I was eventually asked to resign. Tearfully leaving the facility, I had faith that it was time to move on, but no idea what to do next. "Coincidentally", my sponsor was leaving her position as an outpatient addiction counselor at a nearby hospital. I *humbly asked God to support and to guide my future development.* Within a couple weeks I was working in the addiction field.

In my third year of recovery I married for the third time. This time I was sober, in love, and chose wisely. I'd always wanted children but had spent years avoiding pregnancy so I could continue to drink and drug. In sobriety, I was healthy, responsible, and felt ready to parent but would I be blessed with the opportunity? Again, I *humbly asked God to support and guide my future development.* I became pregnant within the year. There is something very reassuring in turning one's will and life over. I felt certain all would be well when I conceived my children. I was blessed with healthy children and the power to care for them.

My husband was offered a job in Florida and we were off. In Florida my education qualified me to get licensed as a mental health counselor. Each step of the way, I envisioned the next one and kept an eye out for the door to open. I met someone who knew someone who set me up as a counselor in an outpatient addiction program. Along the way my husband and I visualized, imagining what we wanted. We a*dmitted to God, to ourselves and another human being the exact nature of our potential as sober individuals.* The more details we added to our treasure map, the easier it was to move towards our goals. By believing we could own a house, we did. By believing we could each start a business, we did. By believing I could complete a Ph.D., I did. Exhilarated by increasing success and my growing family, I kept forging ahead. Unfortunately, my husband did not.

We struggled to preserve the relationship. Three separate periods of marriage counseling and seven years of effort left us exhausted. Despite my sobriety, I had become angry, irritable and discontent. Eventually I realized that holding tightly to the fantasy that the marriage could survive was violating the 9$_S$th Step, *became willing to execute those plans whenever possible except when to do so might interfere with our recovery. I made a decision to turn my will and my life over to the care of God as I understand God.* God did for me what I would not do for myself. It became imperative to file for divorce.

Single again, there was chaos everywhere. An employee had stolen my identity while I was distracted with family matters. Both children were struggling with the break-up of our family. There were many bills and several mortgages. *I sought through prayer and meditation to improve my conscious contact with God, as I understand God, praying only for the knowledge of God's will for me and the power to carry that out.* How to do it? ODAT – One day at a time! Just believing that it could be possible kept me focused on making it possible.

2005 was the worst year of my life. I was 24 years clean and sober and wanted to drink. Personal growth was put aside. I recognized to continue trying to move forward *might interfere with my recovery.* It was back to basics. I went to meetings and hunkered down with the original 12 steps supplemented with Al-Anon. After a year I *had a spiritual experience as the result of these steps* and I was again ready to *make a list of goals and plans I envisioned for my future.* I once again *admitted to God, to myself and another human being the exact nature of my potential as a sober individual* and began to move forward with my career. My daughter was able to recover her focus and resurrect her career path. My son married and had a son, creating his own family when ours disbanded. I have continued *to turn my will, my life, and the lives of those I love over to the care of God as I understand God.*

Having discovered the power to manage my life, having been restored to sanity, recognizing my assets, talents and capabilities, I was blessed with even greater personal growth. My professional life is rich and diverse. I am privileged to help others who still suffer. When I renewed my active involvement in recovery groups, I noticed many people with long term sobriety felt something was missing. What was different? I wondered. Why didn't I feel the same way? With that, I realized I had taken my recovery beyond doing the 12 Steps as they were originally written. I had adapted them as described in this book. Recognizing that I had, indeed, *had a spiritual experience as a result of these steps,* I knew I must *carry this message to others so they might also continue to grow and improve their lives.* That was the point at which I knew I must write this book. It is written as part of my continued growth with profound gratitude for the 12 Steps, both as originally written and in their inverse, this sequel.

ENDNOTES

PREFACE

1. For example: *Narcotics Anonymous Basic Text* (World Services Office, 2008) or *Alcoholics Anonymous* (Alcoholics Anonymous World Services, Inc., 2001).

INTRODUCTION

2. The Sequel steps will be denoted throughout the text with a subscript s, for example: 1_s 2_s 3_s etc.

3. Here and throughout this book the term "sober" will be used to refer to abstinence from addictive behavior whether the addiction be alcohol, drugs, gambling, work, food or any other substance or behavior that has become compulsive to the degree that it interferes with day-to-day-functioning.

4. The original 12 Steps may be found on pages 59-60 of *Alcoholics Anonymous* (Alcoholics Anonymous World Services, Inc., 2001)

STEP 2_s

5. It may also be helpful if the therapist is a trained trauma specialist. For many, getting sober and looking back at what happened due to addiction is traumatic.

6. The use of the term, God, is for convenient reference to the 12 step theistic foundation. If you do not believe in a supreme deity or prefer not to use the Christian term, please substitute a reference you

prefer. The author makes no presumption that there is a God but only that there is a higher power. Read on to Chapters 3 and 11 for further discussion.

7. The original Steps used the masculine pronoun, Him, to denote God. That has been replaced here to allow more diverse definitions of God.

8. FAA is the acronym for the Federal Aviation Administration the national aviation authority in the United States.

9. TSA is the acronym for the Transportation Security Administration responsible to protect the transportation systems in the United States.

10. In some parts of the world, newcomers to AA are referred to as "babies" to denote the rebirth that comes with recovery from alcoholism.

11. A Christian movement initiated by an American Lutheran pastor, Dr. Frank Buchman, popular during the 1920's and 1930's.

12. Personal communication with the author, June 2002.

STEP 3$_S$

13. This expression is often used in 12 Step rooms. I first heard it from Gene R at the Chip House, a halfway house for alcoholics in the center of Baltimore City. Gene would stand at the podium and challenge a motley group of addicts in various stages of recovery not to let their hang-ups about God send them out of recovery and back to the streets.

STEP 5$_S$

14. Joseph Campbell is often quoted for saying, "Follow your bliss." "Find where it is, and don't be afraid to follow it." The Power of Myth, pp. 120, 149.

STEP 6_S

15. Socionics, the MBTI assessment, and the Keirsey Temperament Sorter are all based on Jung's typology. If you have taken any of these tests, you may wish to review the results. While generally the results are reasonably stable over a lifetime, if you took the tests during active addiction they may not be representative of your sober self.

16. It is estimated that 75% of the population is more extraverted than introverted. As a minority, introverts are different than the majority and may be seen as lacking social skill. This is usually not the case but rather simply reflects a need for more alone time.

BIBLIOGRAPHY

Alcoholics Anonymous World Services, Inc. (2001). *Alcoholics Anonymous, 4th edition.* New York: Alcoholics Anonymous World Services, Inc.

Alcoholics Anonymous World Services, Inc. (2001). *Twelve Steps and Twelve Traditions.* New York, New York, USA: Alcoholics Anonymous World Services, Inc.

Carnegie, D. (1951). *How To Stop Worrying, And Start Living.* London: World's Work Ltd., London, 1951.

Covey, S. R. (1989). *The 7 Habits of Highly Effective People.* New York: Simon & Schuster.

Dyer, W. W. (1989). *You'll See It When You Believe It: The Way To Your Personal Transformation.* New York: HarperCollins.

Jung, C. G. (1921). *Psychological Types, Collected Works, Volume 6.* Princeton: Princeton University Press.

Kennedy, J. F. (1963, June 25). Address in the Assembly Hall at Paulskirche. Frankfurt, Germany.

Maslow, A. (1954). *Motivation and Personality.* New York: Harper and Row.

Miller, W.R. & Harris, R.J. (2000). A simple scale of Gorski's warning signs for relapse.Journal of Studies on Alcohol, 759-765.

Myklebust, M. & Wunder, J. (2010). *Healing Foods Pyramid.* Retrieved March 24, 2012, from University of Michigan Integrative Medicine: http://www.med.umich.edu/umim/food-pyramid/dark_chocolate.htm

Narcotics Anonymous. (1986). Just for Today. *Little White Booklet* .

Partridge, S. F. (1951). How To Stop Worrying, And Start Living. In D. Carnegie.

Piper, W. (1976). *The Little Engine That Could.* New York: Platt & Munk.

Ryan, R. & Deci, E.L. (2000). Self-Determination Theory and the Facilitation of Intrinsic Motivation, Social Development, and Well-being. *American Psychologist* , 68-78.

Seligman, M.E.P. & Csikszentmihaly, M. (2000). Positive Psychology: An Introduction. *American Psychologist* , 5-14.

Seuss, D. (1990). *Oh, the Places You'll Go.* New York: Random House.

Sharma, A. M. (2006). *Exercise for Mental Health.* Retrieved March 24, 2012, from Primary Care Companion to the Journal of Clinical Psychiatry: http://www.ncbi.nlm.nih.gov/pmc/articles/PMC1470658/

The Holy Bible, New International Version. (2011). Biblica.

Williamson, M. (1992). *A Return to Love.* New York: Harper Perennial.

Wilson, B. (1958). The Next Frontier: Emotional Sobriety. *AA Grapevine.*

World Services Office. (2008). *Narcotics Anonymous Basic Text, 6th Edition.* Van Nuys: CA: World Service Office.

Made in the USA
San Bernardino, CA
09 June 2015